CAPITALIZING ON EDUCATION IN EMERGENCIES IN SOUTH SUDAN

THE PERSPECTIVES FROM THE SILENT CRISES

ABRAHAM MABIOR RIOC MANYANG
M. Ed., M. Ed., & B. Ed.

Critical Acclaim

"This book will tend out to be a brilliant piece of writing which is worth reading and recommended to all educational stakeholders, scholars, teachers, Education and Child project officers, Education Managers and coordinators working for NGOs to keep it in handy. The author offered a great in-depth analysis and professional insightfulness that can help in scaling up EiE in the fragile nation-states."

Dr. Edward Momo (RIP), Former Dean of the School of Education, University of Juba - South Sudan

"The credibility of this book will stretch or plaster such EiE gaps that occur in our educational process, given many emergencies that always come our way. This book must come to light for its worth since it expounds a new field and alternative means to continue with learning process during emergencies, will be a welcomed discovery."

Ustaz Lewis Anei Madut-Kuendit, Former Governor of Warrap State, Professional Educationist, Author, Culturalist, Politician and Influential Writer - South Sudan

"Ustaz Abraham Mabior Rioc, offers an exceptional contribution in the field of Education in Emergencies that will help the present and the next sets of generations to advance the real-world approaches to Education in the times of Crises. He explains in details the key everyday attitudes and strategies that can help to improve the education system in the face of predicaments and I highly recommend it for readers from different facets of specializations."

Rev. Sr. Georgina Victor Abingkwaec, Head of Education, Catholic University of South Sudan - South Sudan.

"The book, therefore, makes a range of observations on the realities of Education in Emergencies in the country. This book is therefore highly recommended to South Sudanese, other Africans, and educationists worldwide to enable them understand the meaning of Education in Emergencies in a country."

Professor Sibrino Barnaba Forojalla, Department of Educational Planning and Management & Education in Emergencies (EiE), School of Education, University of Juba

Review: "This book is an easy and informative read for anyone who is interested in learning more about the Education in Emergencies (EiE). Although, this book focuses solely on South Sudan, it provides comparisons and perspectives that offers great depth in understanding the challenges of emergency in other developing countries which are also going through a similar political trajectory. The author has done an excellent job in detailing historical and cultural factors that affect provision of education in emergencies and what can be done to increase and improve the level of education despite war and conflict. This book provides great insight into the current and potential challenges faced by South Sudanese students and teachers alike in the pursuit of education.

Dedication

This book is dedicated to all the people affected by the lack of Education in Emergencies at the global level!

A Note from the Publisher

The publisher wishes to acknowledge and thank Dr Douglas H. Johnson for his invaluable help and support for Africa World Books and its mission of preserving and promoting African cultural and literary traditions and history. Dr Johnson and fellow historians have been instrumental in ensuring that African people remain connected to their past and their identity. Africa World Books is proud to carry on this mission.

© *Abraham Mabior Rioc,* 2022

ISBN: 9780645398854

All rights reserved.

All rights reserved. No part of this publication may be reproduced, stored in a retrieval system, or transmitted in any form or by any means, mechanical, photocopying, recording, scanning, or otherwise, without prior written permission to the Publisher or the Author, or authorization through the payment of the appropriate fee per copy to the author.

This book is sold subject to the conditions that it shall not, by way of trade or otherwise, be lent, re-sold, hired out or otherwise circulated without the publisher's prior consent in any form of binding or cover other than in which it is published and without a similar condition including the condition being imposed on the subsequent purchaser.

Cover design, typesetting and layout : Africa World Books

TABLE OF CONTENTS

Acknowledgments	*ix*
List of Abbreviations and Acronyms	*xiii*
Foreword	*xvii*
Preface	*xxiii*
Part One: Introduction	1
Part Two: The Importance of Education in the Times Of Crises	36
Part Three: Negative Impressions Toward Education in the Times of Crises	55
Part Four: Considering Education as a Shared Responsibility	99
Part Five: Conceptualizing Teacher Professional Development in the Times of Crises	148
Part Six: Measurement and Assessment of the Learning Endeavors	168
Part Seven: School Safety and Disaster Risk Reduction (DRR)	180
Part Eight: Conclusions and Personal Reflections	192
Glossary	*209*
References	*215*
About the Author	*219*

ACKNOWLEDGMENTS

Most importantly, I thank Almighty God, the Creator of the Universe and Grantor of life, for being my close protector and guide in the pursuit of my social, academic, and professional aspirations. Though this book was single-handedly put together and compiled by myself, it is my pleasure to acknowledge the countless contributions and virtuous sustenance of many people who shared with me their distinctive facets of life in terms of moral, financial, and professional support.

From the deepest part of my heart, I am humbly indebted and earnestly thankful to Gen. Akol Koor Kuc, the Director-General of the Internal Security Bureau (ISB) at the National Security Services (NSS), for his kindness to raise eighty percent of the financial contribution to support the publication of this book. On the same note, I am extremely thankful and credibly appreciative to Hon. Mayiik Ayii Deng, the former Minister of Presidential Affairs and now the Minister of Foreign Affairs and International Cooperation, for extending his financial backing in support of the publication of this book. On this sincere basis, I straightforwardly recognize and appreciate their senses of humanity to provide financial support for this book to see the light of the day.

On equal terms, I would like to express my profound gratitude and thanks to Prof. Julia Aker Duany, the Undersecretary of the Ministry of Public Services and Human Resource Development and who is on top of that, the founder of the Gender Equity and Women's Leadership Program (GEWLP). I sincerely thank her for initiating a USAID-fully funded Master of Education in Emergencies at the University of Juba, to which my colleagues and I turned out to be immediate beneficiaries and in the end became direct scholars. Without such a worthwhile academic and capable platform, the idea of writing this book could have not been planned and implemented.

Equally significant, I am so much thankful to the family of Open Society Foundations (OSF) for offering me a full postgraduate scholarship through Civil Society Leadership Awards (CSLA) to expand my professional knowledge in the field of education. Indeed, the offer of such a distinctive scholarship helped in advancing my professional and teaching career pathways in the education to pursue a Master of Education in Comparative and Global Studies in Education and Development from The University of Hong Kong. Without a doubt, both master's programs have made a sharp turning point in my social, moral, intellectual, and professional life.

On the other hand, I am indebted to Prof. Sibrino Barnaba Forojalla for writing the foreword of this book. Being the first lecturer to introduce me to the course of Education in Emergencies, I was able to pick a considerable interest from his EiE-designed lectures, which enabled me to write and compile this book. His scholarship, professional dedication and support have shaped my love for education and sharpened my professional thinking towards EiE in a colossal stand. I am also indebted to Mr. Peter Lual Deng, the Founder of the African World Books Education Community and his team for their tireless efforts to edit, design, and publish the book as well as giving their instrumental advice.

On the contrary, I am obliged to my frontal professors in the personalities of Prof. John Apuruot Akec, the Vice-Chancellor of the University of Juba and the former Dean of the School of Education, Dr Edward Momo Yakobo (RIP) for encouraging me to publish the book. I am also indebted to my former lecturers from the School of Education, Ustaz Ben Saliba Lagure, Ustaz John Richard Otema, the Acting Dean of the School of Education, Dr Awad Kherilla Hassan, and Dr Natania Baya

Yosa, who encouraged me to compile my knowledge into a book for public consumption. I am also grateful to professors from Indiana University, Dr Kathryn Engebretson and Dr Maria Hamilton Abegunde, for encouraging me to advance my professional career in the field of Education. Thank you for having groomed me professionally and influenced my thinking to love education unreservedly.

In a similar vein, I am equally indebted to Ustaz Lewis Anei Madut-Kuendit for his invaluable advice, intellectual remarks, and encouragement to apply my knowledge to write books so that the current and next set of generations may benefit from my knowledge. Ustaz Lewis Aneidit has always been a guiding star to mentor, advice and encourage young people to pursue their varied academic and professional endeavors for the good of the society. In the same way, I sincerely thank Maj. Gen. Majok Michael Chan, the former Commandant of Ngachigak Military College and who is now the Chief of General Training of the South Sudan People's Defense Forces (SSPDF), for releasing me with pay to pursue my undergraduate on one hand. On the other hand, I thank him for giving me another opportunity to pursue my two different postgraduate studies one on-one basis. Without his tender heart and kindness to allow me to complete my university education, this book could have not been written and published.

By the same token, I sincerely extend my appreciation and thanks to my long-time colleagues and mentors in the personalities of Col. Peter Akech Liai Angok, Captain Benjamin Muorwel Manin, Mr. Daniel Deng Deng-Maker, Eng. Marial Deng Mathiang, Eng. Kuc Mayur Kuc, Ustaz William Deng Cirrillo Chol, Diplomat Mathiang Beny Til, Dr Kur Bona Bol Abur, Dr Matueny Muorwel Matueny, Ustaz Santino Majok Madut, and others for having supported me morally to pursue my professional aspirations. In addition, I am equally thankful to my uncle, Ustaz Ireneo Mapuol Mapuol and colleagues in the persons of Dr Mawien Deng Deng, Mr. George Agok Mayar, Dr Mawien Maring Kuol, Maj. Peter Majok Mou, Maj. Muoter Mouter Akot, 2nd Lt. Giir Athuai Yak, Mr. John Chol Deng-Malek, Eng. James Goch Wol, Eng. Charles Machar Nhial Machar, Mr. Mario Maker Majok, and the list is overly long. I sincerely thank them for their persistent advice and guidance in the course of pursing this mind-numbing writing job besides my career pathways.

Furthermore, I am equally indebted to my academic friend and scholar Ustaz John Garang Ayii Riak, for his scholarly contributions in the field of Education in Emergencies and our interactive conversations in light of critical issues hampering EiE in South Sudan. I equally recognize the scholarly roles and advice shared with me by my former postgraduate mates and scholars across different universities and among them include Ustaz Chan Reath, Ustaz Batheng Babouth, Ustaz Peter Manyang Biar, Rev. Sr. Georgina Victor Abingkwaec and others for encouraging me to write this book for the good use of the public.

By the same token, I am also indebted to Hon. Tong Deng Anei, the former State Minister of Health and former State Minister of Culture, Youth and Sports for the Government of Northern Bahr el Ghazal, for providing a photo of school learners, which has been used as a cover page for this book.

Last but not least, I am thankful and appreciative to the readers of the original manuscript and more especially to those who acclaimed the book's credibility as one of the groundbreaking books of the Education in Emergencies. At the last moment, I thank all my family members, colleagues, and friends for valuable suggestions and ideas to be considered in this book. Once again, I thank everyone for being there for me through thick and thin!

LIST OF ABBREVIATIONS AND ACRONYMS

21st: Twenty-First Century
2nd Lt: Second Lieutenant
AAA: Abyei Administrative Area
AES: Alternative Education Program
APM: Assistant Technical Programme Manager
ARCSS: Agreement on the Resolution of Conflict in South Sudan
BoG: Board of Governors
CEDs: County Education Directors
CFS: Child-Friendly School
Col: Colonel
Covid-19: Coronavirus Disease 2019
CPA: Comprehensive Peace Agreement
CRC: Convention on the Right of the Child
Cs: Century Skills
CSLA: Civil Society Leader Awards
CWD: Children with Disabilities
D.C: District of Columbia
DDR: Disarmament, Demobilization, and Reintegration
DfID: Department of Foreign and International Development
Dr: Doctor
DRR: Disasters Risk Reduction
ECW: Education Cannot Wait
EFA: Education for All
EiE. Education in Emergencies
Eng: Engineer
Gen. General
GEWLP: Gender Equity and Women's Leadership Program
GPAA: Greater Pibor Administrative Area

HIV/AIDS: Human Immunodeficiency Virus/Acquired Immunodeficiency Syndromes
HKSAR: Hong Kong Special Administrative Region
HRW: Human Rights Watch
ICC: International Criminal Court
IGAD. Inter-Governmental Authority on Drought
INEE: Inter-Agency Network for Education in Emergencies
ISB: Internal Security Bureau
J1: Juba One
KPA. Khartoum Peace Agreement
LRA: Lord Resistance's Army
Maj: Major
MDGs: Millennium Development Goals
MEP: Master of Education Project
NSS: National Security Services
OCHA: Office of the Coordination of the Humanitarian Affairs
OSF: Open Society Foundation
Prof: Professor
PSS: Psychosocial Support Services
PTAs: Parents Teachers' Associations
R-ARCSS: Revitalized Agreement on the Resolution of Conflict in South Sudan
RIP: Rest in Peace
RoE: Rules of Engagement
SCI: Save the Children International
SEA: Sexual Exploitation and Abuse
SIDA: The Swedish International Development Cooperation Agency
SMC: School Management Committee
SE: School of Education
SPLA: Sudan People's Liberation Army
SPLM/A: Sudan People's Liberation Movement/Army
SPLM/IO: Sudan People's Liberation Movement in Opposition

SSLM: South Sudan Liberation Movement
SSNLM: South Sudan National Liberation Movement
SSPDF: South Sudan People's Defense Forces
STEM: Sciences, Technology, Engineering, and Mathematics
TLS: Temporary Learning Space
TPD: Teacher Professional Development
UK: United Kingdom
UKAID: United Kingdom Agency for International Development
UN: United Nations
UNCRC: United Nations Convention on the Rights of the Child
UNESCO: United Nations Educational, Scientific and Cultural Organization
UNICEF: United Nations' Children Fund
UNSCR: United Nations Security Council Resolution
USA: United States of America
USAID: The United States Agency for International Development
USAID: United States Agency for International Development
WASH: Water, Sanitation, and Hygiene

FOREWORD

Education in Emergencies (EiE), is comparatively, a new concept and academic program in the field of Education. In the past decades, many leading scholars had typically written and presented their papers to separate educational conferences and academic forums to have EiE be recognized. In addition, especially in recent years, the idea of EiE was consequently advanced and persistently advocated by a scholar and journalist, Jackie Kirk. Her brilliant ideas were more widely publicized after her death by two of her friends and colleagues, Karen Mundy and Sarah Dryden-Peterson. Both academic friends carefully edited the book as an eloquent tribute to her, titled, *Educating Children in Conflict Zones: Research, Policy and Practice for Systematic Change,* published by Teacher College Press, University of Colombia, in New York (2011). The publication was launched a year earlier in 2010 by Kevin Cahill in the book entitled "Even in chaos: Education in Times of Emergency", published by Fordham University Press. This book has immensely underscored the paramount importance of EiE to be universally recognized as a vital tool to be typically employed to save learners and school personnel during the crises.

The published book by Mundy and Dryden-Petersen exposes the considerable difficulties encountered by pupils, students and teachers in what is termed as the 'Fragile States.' Fragile state is also rather a controversial term. Nonetheless, it is one of the easiest working definitions to be used globally. Fragile State refers to the *"state where the government cannot or will not deliver core functions to the majority of its people, including the poor"* (DfID), the UK's Department of Foreign and International Development, which is occasionally opposed by principal leaders of the affected fragile states. Likewise, Cahill customarily publishes concrete cases of these problems and challenges encountered by students and teachers particularly females, during a crisis situation in such countries.

Following the acknowledged genesis of the Master of Education in Emergencies at the University of Juba, the idea to establish such a rare field of study was brought up for discussion after the 2013 political crisis in South Sudan. In 2016, the academic staff of both Faculties of Education, University of Indiana, USA, and University of Juba, South Sudan had forged the academic cooperation to develop a curriculum for a Master's degree program in Education in Emergencies. The academic cooperation turned out to be a reality and a project was inked to start the Master of Education in Emergencies.

This successful project came to be popularly known as Master of Education Project (MEP), located at the School of Education of the University of Juba. The master's program was directed jointly by the faculties of education from both universities with financial support from the United States Agency for International Development (USAID). The focus of the program is to help form a corps of skilled and capable educators to address the needs of schools, teachers and students pursuing education amidst conflict and its aftermath. In addition, MEP is also meant to support South Sudanese people to create a sustainable South Sudanese-led program at University of Juba's College of Education so that the future generations of university-trained school teachers and academic administrators can strengthen South Sudan's education sector, raise literacy rates and narrow the gender gap, bringing more women and girls into classrooms around the country.

Over the recent decades, through the prolonged liberation struggle for equality within Sudan from 1955 through 2005, the then South Sudanese people experienced serious emergency education situations. Regrettably, after independence in 2011, the crisis has continued thoughtfully in South Sudan as a result of internal civil wars and communal conflicts. These distressing conflicts were invariably triggered by differences amongst political and cultural leaders. As a result, South Sudanese communities continue to vicariously experience the objective reality of education in emergencies, perhaps more than any other African countries.

The author of the present book, "Capitalizing on Education in Emergencies in South Sudan: The Perspective from the Silent Crises" (2021), was amongst the first batch of MEP students who graduated from the College of Education, University of Juba. He was amongst the brilliant students who benefited from the program with quality education and professional aspirations to advance their education with a core aim to impact the local communities. Although the program was meant for girls to promote female gender education, he was among the fortunate few male students to be considered for the scholarship.

Moreover, there were considerable enthusiasm and effort by the academic staff, both from Juba and Indiana, to lay a sound foundation for the program. This was enhanced by the generous and financial support from the USAID to fund Master of Education in Emergencies, School of Education of the University of Juba. For children in all sorts of emergencies, education is considered to be more than the right to acquire and survive. In fact, it is a well-thought idea that schools protect children from the physical dangers around them like an abuse, exploitation and recruitment into armed groups. On faithful grounds, EiE provides children with lifesaving messages and life-sustaining information, clean drinking water, health care and hygienic supplies.

Prior to taking part in the master's degree studies, the author of this book, Abraham Mabior Rioc, had undergone practical realities of education in the country. He has authored scholarly and cultural articles in different media outlets enlightening his people across the country and beyond about the importance of education. This book, therefore, offers a range of observations on the realities of education in emergencies in the country.

More importantly, this book highlights the apparent impacts of emergency such as the occupation of schools by soldiers and other fighting forces. In addition, the book underscores the threat to school girls, young women and female teachers, parents, as well as teachers in general in times of crises. The overall result is the disadvantageous situation of female students, forced into early marriage by parents as a way of protection. In spite of that, this is considered worse by traditions where girls are considered as a source of wealth and are therefore compulsory forced into early and obligatory marriages.

In the case of teachers, their voluntary offers to teach their young community members have been worsened by the moderate level of education and uncertain payment of salaries, even when they are employed. This is, however, prevalent through the comprehensive education system and is a discouragement to the teaching profession. It is sad to bear in mind that EiE, has no legal importance and social recognition in the national system of education, particularly in the context of South Sudan. However, it is worthwhile to mention that EiE helps learners to gain equitable access to safe, quality and recognized basic and tertiary education for all. It is also imperative the programs for Education in Emergencies should focus on helping children who are out of school to be enrolled back to the learning system for quality education to succeed all year in and out.

On the other hand, the role of education partners, drawn by the leading cause of education in emergencies, is offering a range of support. The roles should also consider TPD programming activities, such as proactive pre-service and in-service. Merely, in-service and pre-service teacher training programs by which teachers engage in further education or training to refresh or upgrade their professional knowledge, skills and practices in the course of their gainful employment.

Deliberately, EiE should encompass formal teacher professional development programs to strengthen the essential quality of teaching activities. These formal TPD activities are typically defined as learning experiences for teachers that are persistently designed to support particular kinds of teacher change. These may also include an intensive and multiday session for teachers that takes place outside of the teacher's classroom or within the school environment. Teacher professional development program is an important milestone to ensure teacher competency framework is adequately realized.

Under some common learning formalities, other capacity-building programs such as advocacy for inclusive education approaches and gender sensitivity should also be taken into consideration during crises. Along the similar lines, conflict mitigation or conflict resolution skills, peace education, water and hygiene and sanitation, and child protection are duty-bound to take considerable preference in the times of crises. All these continuous speculative lineups are efforts designed to pave the way for quality education to succeed in the country. This book is therefore highly recommended to South Sudanese scholars, other Africans, and educationists worldwide to enable them to intuitively understand the meaning of Education in Emergencies across the fragile states.

By Professor Sibrino Barnaba Forojalla

School of Education, University of Juba
Department of Educational Planning and
Management & Education in Emergencies (EiE),
Author of the Book entitled:
"Educational Planning for Development"
Macmillan Publishers, London & Teachers College Press, Columbia University, New York (1993)

PREFACE

My motivation to write this book has been a great labor of love for Education in Emergencies. Out of professional curiosity, the concrete idea that pushed me to compile this book came to mind in 2016 following the bloody hostility that pitted the government forces against the bodyguards of Dr Riek Machar and resulted in a brutal aggression. The inhuman battle came to be popularly known as the J1 (aka Juba One) Dogfight. By that time, I was in my first year of postgraduate study, pursuing a Master of Education in Emergencies in the School of Education at the University of Juba. As the conflict intensified, most learning institutions of all levels of education across the country were instantly interrupted. For instance, the majority of the learning institutions were temporarily closed down and destroyed. Other learning midpoints were momentarily occupied by the armed forces, especially those located outside Juba. This presented an undesired outcome for learners specifically and the education system in general.

Needless to say, massive internal and external displacement of people ensued, and most of the learning institutions across the country were brought to a complete standstill. Consequently, insecurity tended out to be the leading consequence for interruption of schooling since it affected both the learners and their parents. At the initial stages of confrontation, many tertiary institutions operating in Juba, including our university were in the short term interrupted. From the onset, my mind was engaged to believe that teaching and learning institutions should not be interrupted by any emergency. The overriding paradigm shift is that disruptions of the teaching and learning activities without government interventions may lead to indefinable educational wastage. As a result, this may as well upset the learners and the parents respectively. Thus, the whole consequence of conflict definitely leads to a depressing impact on the national education system in terms of a low numeracy and literacy boost.

In this regard, I had to recuperate my thoughts and ideas to write a practical book that underscores the importance of providing education during crises. In light of this critical outlook on EiE, I have to elaborate on the key impacts related to the non-operationalization of learning institutions. As the result of the disconnection of learning and teaching accomplishments in the face of crises, major negative impacts tend to override the performance of the education system. Although this book was initially designed to focus on the importance of education and impact of emergencies in times of crises, some critical topics which can support education in time of crises were encompassed.

In light of this educational reality check, I was able to factor in some important elements of education such as continuous teacher professional development, school safety and disaster risk reduction, and measurement and evaluation of learning accomplishments. Figuratively, the scope of the book was expanded to include central intervention strategies in form of collective responsibilities among education actors, the government, and the broader humanitarian community to protect children during crises while in the school settings. Having suggested the continuity of educational activities in the face of crisis as an inspiring key, in this way, protecting schools is a distinguished social discourse to be worthily supported by all.

In an average concept, emergency of any types receives negative consequences on the lives of human beings across the globe. Within the term of emergency, I also recall the underlying concept of 'Emergency' that is used almost in any situations that are unfavorable. For instance, an emergency could be a serious, unexpected, and often dangerous situation which may call for immediate actions. In addition, an emergency is a situation that poses an imminent risk to human health and life and their property, and even to the surrounding environment itself. Indeed, most emergencies alternatively seek for urgent intervention to prevent a worsening of the situation. Although in some situations, efforts of mitigation may not be possible and supportive agencies may only be effective to offer palliative care for in the aftermath of the crises. However, the government or the authority concerned is expected to issue some immediate emergency measures which are aimed at adequately managing the situation.

By referring back to my more initial years of military physical fitness activities in 2003 at Ngop Military Training Center, emergency was a harsh term when call to mind. Subsequently in Owinykibul Military College in 2012, it reminded me of emergency calls we were physically exposed to as a form of military training exercise to learn and control any looming danger. As trainees, we were introduced and exposed to an emergency call exercise on frequently basis. In its virtual context, an emergency call is a practical military term used by the military trainers and the army to rouse the attention of soldiers to any danger besetting the military units. It has some sound signals such as blowing whistles satirically and repeatedly, beating drums, and rhythm all sorts of metallic items. For instance, such emergency warnings could be declared when military raids, ambushes, or offensive attacks are framed by the enemies at any time and space. In its very nature, we were exposed to panic and worrying situations to which our normal activities could be momentarily interposed and disorganized. This is a training experience that is introduced to military trainees since it is similar to what may happen in one's real life situations in the future.

By way of moving towards city life and within the context of expanding education considerably, I feel that an emergency should be dealt with in a collective manner in the event that it strikes unexpectedly. As a scholar who has specialized in EiE, the idea of writing a book about education in emergencies tended to be ignited and virtually adopted along the similar lines of past experiences. As a diligent postgraduate student, especially in the course of studying for my two distinctive master's degrees, I had to spare my limited time and energy to compile a few texts and save them in a manuscript format for that matter. From my viewpoint, if such dire situations happen in a large and busy learning environment, one can merely imagine the rough and destructive moment of crises that ought to be controlled by the concerned leadership.

In this practical reverence of crisis, it has become very clear that an emergency is a disastrous situation that needs immediate intervention. Definitely, such interventional efforts should be inform of providing energetic educational strategies to be applied for the best alternative and effective response mechanisms. Therefore, this may restraint us from overlooking the importance of education during emergency. The real-world inference about EiE is that the domestic government agencies should shift the focus from relying on donors, but to advance their domestic socio-economic commitments toward education. This commitment should be considerate to realize quality and relevant educational opportunities for all learners during the emergency and non-emergency contexts.

From a relative standpoint, education is the right to be unreservedly given to the citizens during emergency and non-emergency contexts. As such, the government should change the course of direction and focus on relevant education system which can answer community needs in the face of crises. In a simple approach, part of the practical solution lies in the kind of education we should admire and the strategies to be availed during crises in order to enable a positive and child-friendly learning environment. The point I am driving here is that activities that encourage the continuity and progress of learning at all levels of education should be made substantially appealing to both the learners and their parents or guardians. Constructively, my institutional argument focuses on redirecting education in emergencies to consider the accessibility, desirability and affordability of educational opportunities by all learners regardless of political, economic, geographic, and demographic affiliations.

Through my consistency and persistence to make sure that the book could see the light of the day, I was able to analyze and evaluate the unfolding situations of educational activities in many parts of South Sudan. In fact, aligning myself to analyze different situations gave me a wider geographic and demographic understanding of the nature of EiE to be offered and collectively desired by the learners. Without a doubt, EiE demands serious institutional attention especially in the provision of Temporary Learning Spaces (TLS) as a quick impactful intervention that supports meaningful continuity of learning. This can be followed with the provision of appropriate learning furniture and materials to afford an enabling learning environment for all learners. To an extent, this may help the teaching force to create student-learning plans that are aimed at supporting individual and cooperative learning environments for the success of the whole education system.

As the development of ideas that constituted this book ensured, I took a critical look at the current educational activities and practical evaluation of the challenges facing teachers and the students during the crisis. To this end, I seized a real-world approach to present ideas in a more conversant and stress-free reading and understanding styles. This is to enable the readers to understand and appreciate the performance of EiE and internalize the significant educational concepts in light of the provision of quality educational services.

The main goal of the book is to provide practical guidelines and better compassions for education in emergencies to overrule the public and private learning institutions. Fundamentally, this gives educators a specific knowledge on the provision of quality educational services in the face of crises. This essentially creates knowledge curiosity for the learning curves of the students to be consistently maintained and enthusiastically elevated. From a global outlook, EiE has been gaining substantial attention from educational settings around the globe and specifically the developing countries. In detail, some countries have been described by a state of fragility, and this is coupled with the destruction availed by man-made and naturally occurring phenomena.

To a larger extent, this book has been specifically written for practice and prospective dons and education policy-makers. On the same note, this book is virtually intended to serve as a resource and a guide for education officers, school inspectors and administrators. Likewise, this book will be a handbook tool for education project officers, education program coordinators and managers working for NGOs, teachers, and the practicing teaching force. Generally speaking, it is a worthy read for all scholars across different professions and more specially the students, both undergraduate and postgraduate of education and Social Sciences. Alternatively, this book could remain a vibrant apparatus to be used by pre-service and in-service teachers to support teaching and learning activities both during the emergency and non-emergency contexts. This will help to improve the quality of educational services through acceptable means on effective delivery of learning contents during crises.

From a different perspective, the book can also be useful for different educational settings in terms of school leadership and the contributions from the government, community, and well-wishers. Indeed, effective institutional leadership continues to be a central point for managing meritorious day-to-day affairs of the learning institutions. In social adaptation to support learning, this brings us to a closer understanding and appreciation of different stakeholders and development actors to prioritize EiE and support its operationalization from urban to the community peripheries.

Optimistically, this book will bring a desired educational change in the way people look at educational activities in South Sudan, as they call for our collective accountabilities from the start to the end. It is specifically designed to encourage and support educators in the difficult task of providing quality learning opportunities during crises. In doing so, can improve the country's education system to reach maximum excellence in the teaching and learning endeavors that are bound to produce the best educational standards and learning outcomes.

This book, to the best of my knowledge, is the first of its kind in South Sudan. Practically, this book draws many-sided experiences from a variety of sources in relation to the shared role and responsibilities for both the government, school leadership, the community, and the international education actors. In addition, the intention of the book is to provide groundbreaking knowledge and a workable approach for constructing a comfortable and supportive learning environment appropriate for all learning activities during crises. It is within my earnest hope that the abstract ideas and practical solutions presented in this book will give educators the prospective notions to explore, in-depth and breadth, the necessity to expand educational opportunities during emergency context.

Part One, this book underscores the brief introduction of geographical, political, emergency and educational contexts. The education system of South Sudan is basically drizzling to which I presume to be least relevant subsystem in responding to community needs. I call it a subsystem of a total social system because it has been underperforming since independence up to this point in time. Yet, ordinary citizens are so enthusiastic to attain and maximize the academic and professional performance of their education system. This objectively implies the realization of the intended and set educational goals for the improvement of society during the emergency and non-emergency contexts.

Part Two, the importance of education in emergencies has been discussed extensively and elaborately. For this reason, it exhausted that EiE is an integral component to supplement the educational activities in shaping human capacity and mitigating conflict in the face of crises. The implication of treating EiE as a central element is based on the harsh reality that education could be provided anywhere and at any time even with or without the emergence of crises. From my suggestive standpoint, all what education requires during crises, is to utilize wisely and responsibly the meager resources at the disposal of the concerned authority to realize the bigger goal of education. Obviously, this will reinforce the national education system to be effectively and efficiently functioning. On this broad account, this calls for creating a supportive approach to transmit knowledge and skills to the learners through the provision of the marginal learning alongside the humanitarian and resilient services.

As far as education in an emergency is concerned, it should be mentioned that crises of all sorts have become rampant in human history. As a result, these endless crises routinely affect the normalcy of the school community and its educational activities. Though the degree and level of damage and loss of the school property are not always the same in all emergency contexts, it should be mentioned that the consequences at some points become very devastating to human lives and destructive to people's property. This book substantially itemizes the reality checks on the importance of EiE to be used as a reliable tool to advance socio-economic and conflict mitigation. This part particularizes much on the importance of education in relation to providing psychosocial support programs and counseling activities for both the learners and the teaching forces. Basically, EiE has always been emphasized as one of the key factors for the investment of human resource development.

Remarkably, I believe that education on awareness-raising

grounds, can also mitigate conflict through peaceful interventions to build peaceful and sustainable communities. As a worthwhile tool, education is used to mitigate conflict in a variety of ways between the warring parties including the members of the society who have lost trust and hope in the future and in their leaders as well. This has been itemized by Cahill (2010) that education promotes conflict resolution and peace, social cohesion, tolerance, and respect for human rights. Specifically, education plays multiple roles in the reconstruction of post-conflict societies and healing of sad memories of conflicts. This is by bringing together the parties to the conflicts under one umbrella to compromise their political and economic demands for the sake of peace and unity of the suffering civil population.

Generally speaking, it should be noted that providing EiE revitalizes socio-economic stability and restores a peace of mind among the crisis-affected communities. On this EiE version of realities, the rotten social fabrics and social structures are restructured in society. In this respect, the best needs of the people are met as well as respect for human rights and personal dignity is restored through the fair application of the rule of laws. On the other hand, Culbertson and Constant (2015) believe that a school building strategy should include facilitating both the short-term and long-term scenarios such as repurposing of school buildings, constructing new ones, and availing innovative finance. Collaboratively, the activities for scaling up global and regional long-term funding commitments could be secured to support educational initiatives and programs for the betterment of the affected communities.

Part Three of the book explores much of the content on the basis of the negative impact of armed conflict on education. As far as considering education as a basic human right is concerned, the South Sudanese youths and children have been manipulated by their country's political leadership with or without their knowledge. This points to the harsh political reality in relation to the manner in which civil wars have been fought with a large portion of the country's population being youths below 40 years of age. This means that they are being recruited either persuasively or forcefully to implement the interest of their respective leaders. As a result of recruitment, many youths and adults of school-going age could drop out of the school. Thus, their future is potentially undermined and rendered useless for the rest of their future lives. This suggests that the more recruitment of youths and adults into the armed forces, the more their future is potentially ruined and economically rendered less effective.

Part Four discusses the shared and collective responsibilities for all including the government, members of the community, school leadership as well as global education actors. No matter where and how the emergency situations strike, it is important to acknowledge that the varied responsibilities continue to be exclusively taken and administered by the concerned government. It is an undeniable fact that the government is the lead partner and sole provider of basic services including education for all. Nevertheless, it may be marked that all members of the community, school leadership, government agencies, local and international organizations, and the United Nations Agencies are expected to participate either morally, financially, or materially. The government in any given nation-state is seemingly the sole provider of all basic services including maximum security and protection of public resources. Nonetheless, there are some situations where the government fails to execute its noticeable and usual responsibilities. This raises a lot of doubts and questions to anybody who may ask for an obvious clarity that catechizes the role of the government in times of crisis.

Part Five focuses on Teacher Professional Development (TPD) as an important component in education system. Given that education can take place almost anywhere, a safe, accessible and comfortable learning space is an absolute priority. This creates confidence in learners to attend their learning activities in big number. This momentously improves the ability of the teacher to conduct structured content and needs-based learning activities and for students to expressively participate to learn. In an emergency, some learning centers and educational spaces may not be safe, secure, and accessible for a number of reasons. Undeniably, TPD should be designed in order to be contextually relevant to the needs of the communities. Thus, TPD should entice effective learning and teaching activities especially in a crisis where quality education is seriously compromised and professionally ignored.

Ultimately, one of the school leadership roles is to scale up planning with reference to the daily affairs of the school setting. This strategic planning could be adjusted according to situations in order for the schools to run effectively and efficiently. In a learning atmosphere, educational planning suggests an effective alternative to manage educational activities successfully.

Comparatively, the teaching profession remains the lowest valued occupation in South Sudan and perhaps in other parts of the world. However, it could be worsened by the manifestation of any human and natural catastrophes. In more cases, the national resources may be diverted to defense and national security sectors in case of a man-made disaster such as armed conflict. In an effort to help schools stand active and serviceable to communities, teacher training is one of the best tools that helps education zone to achieve its educational goals during an emergency situation.

Part Six focuses on measurement and evaluation of learning activities during crises. It is important to bear in mind that that elements of monitoring and evaluation are simultaneous tools applied to evaluate the worthiness of educational content and learning outcomes. Simply put, monitoring is about checking learning progress against educational plans. At some points, it is termed as terminal evaluation to mean summative performance of education. This assesses the progress made towards the achievement of the pre-determined objectives at the end of the program to provide a critical basis for decisions on the future course of action.

Practically, the assessment findings and recommendations are often used to decide whether or not to adjust the instructions. Alternatively, the findings can be used to judge the learning situation if a new phase of teaching approach should be put under consideration. On one hand, formative assessment involves gauging ongoing progress by identifying learner strengths and weaknesses. This form of assessment can also lead to greater learner achievement if both teachers and learners are able to reflect upon and actively consume the information collected insofar.

On the foreground, academic assessment plays numeral roles in the life of a student. However, some of which they may be more aware of the focus of assessment than others. It is widely accepted that students' learning patterns, educational focus, and allocation of time will be directly influenced by well-thought out assessments. In meaningful learning situations, educational assessment is the process of documenting, usually in measurable terms, knowledge, skills, attitudes and beliefs. The overarching goal of assessment is to focus on the individual learner, the learning community, the institution, and the educational system as a whole.

Part Seven solely focuses on school safety, and Disasters Risk Reduction (DRR) as the noticeable component required during crises. As an emergency strikes, disasters often follow natural and manmade hazard. In the succeeding pages, I have talked clearly about some of the manmade and natural disasters which may have a negative impact on the lives of the community and the environment. As time goes by, there could be disaster risk as a result of the crises. Disaster risk is expressed as the likelihood of loss of life, injuries, collateral damages or destruction, as a result of a disaster which may strike in a given period of time.

Disaster risk is widely recognized as the consequence of the interaction between a threat and the characteristics that make people and places vulnerable and exposed terribly. In other words, there are many types of disasters such as flooding, hurricanes, cyclones, drought, civil wars and community conflicts, just to mention a few.

However, in the context of South Sudan, flooding, famine, outbreak of tropical diseases, man-made wars and intercommunal conflicts represent the most typical destructive elements. Both consequences of disasters have led to the loss of millions of people's lives and their property over an extended period of time. On the other hand, there are different types of assessments required for the functionality of schooling for the realization of quality education.

Part Eight deals with the conclusion and personal reflections of the author in light of the provision of education in emergencies. In this sense, I critically reflect on the roles of the communities, education actors, and the school authorities in complimenting the commitment of the government to address educational issues in times of emergencies. The specific provision of educational opportunities during crises continues to be a disturbing challenge facing the fragile states and other crisis-affected regions. On my strong viewpoint, it may be believed that education acts as a catalyst for peacebuilding and conflict mitigation in all its real-world aspects.

Not to mention, if educational needs-based assessments are conducted and results analyzed properly, assessment information can also serve as a key driver in improving the teaching and learning process to realize quality standards. In general, South Sudan and elsewhere in other war-affected regions, the roles of the governments are obvious as underscored in the domestic and international laws. However, in the context of domestic laws, the legally binding instruments have primarily remained in principles without being practically implemented.

The bottom line anticipation is that education remains the vibrant tool to change the mindsets of nomadic societies which are involved in cattle rustling activities. In addition, education as a safe haven can protect the lives of learners and school communities during crises. In this respect, I labor to highlight the importance and impacts of EiE and other components required to complement quality education during crises. On this account, I will be happy if the wider readership forwards the identified ideas and opinions to be considered in the second edition of this book. Speaking in reference to EiE, the book captured practical aspects of EiE with proven impacts on society, if education is to be collectively seized as a shared responsibility for all.

By Abraham Mabior Rioc (The Author)

PART ONE
Introduction:

The Geographical Context

Geographically, South Sudan is bordered to the north by Sudan, Ethiopia to the east, Uganda and Kenya to the southeast, the Democratic Republic of Congo to the southwest, and the Central African Republic to the west. However, it is still not incredibly fashionable in global maps and major universal drop-down network domains. Disappointedly, many other people from our neighboring countries including some South Sudanese people however, call it Southern Sudan, its known previous name instead of the Republic of South Sudan.

Historically, the Republic of South Sudan officially gained its independence from the rest of the Sudan on July 9th, 2011, after the exercise of an internationally supervised and observed referendum in which South Sudanese people overwhelmingly voted for Separation. The referendum was conducted under the terms of the 2005 Comprehensive Peace Agreement (CPA) that ended the decades of lengthy civil war between the North and the South. From then on, a newborn country was officially declared as one of the World's independent nation-states. South Sudan is the 54th African nation-state and 93rd Member State of the United Nations.

As a requirement, the new nation is obligated to the universality of the United Nations and the values that are enshrined in its Charter are thereby enhanced possibilities of upholding and implementing the respective socio-economic bonds in the letter and spirit. This commitment to different charters firmly deep-root South Sudan to come to be one of the nations in the same way as other Member States with the same rights and responsibilities. Henceforth, the country's administration was fully handed over to the leadership of the Sudan People's Liberation Movement (SPLM), the ruling party to run the day-to-day affairs of the emerging nation. Principally, South Sudan also came to be one of the signatories to other world's legal-abiding instruments and certified charters such as the United Nations Convention on the Rights of the Child (UNCRC), the right to education and others.

Based on the former administrative divisions before the interim period and towards the 2013 crises, South Sudan has been composed of 10 states. However, another political decision was reached in 2015 to increase the number of states to be 28 and again increased to 32 states besides the hotly contested Abyei Administrative Area (AAA) between the two countries of Sudan and South Sudan. As a point in the case, the current peace popularly known as the Revitalized Agreement on the Resolution of Conflict in South Sudan (R-ARCSS) has settled the number of the states by reverting to the former ten states. R-ARCSS also gave the special administrative status to Ruweng and Pibor localities. Though the peace is being implemented, it goes on unclear whether the left-out groups will continue to wage wars or be incorporated into the agreement so as to avoid more bloodshed and suffering of the ordinary citizens.

On a different note, South Sudan comprises of the three regions such as Bahr el Ghazal, Upper Nile and Equatoria. From the administrative viewpoint, it is currently subdivided into ten states and 3 administrative Areas. The states include Eastern Equatoria, Western Equatoria, Central Equatoria, Northern Bahr el Ghazal, Western Bahr El Ghazal, Warrap, Lakes, Unity, Upper Nile, and Jonglei. The three administrative areas include Abyei Administrative Area, Greater Pibor Administrative Area (GPAA), and Ruweng Administrative Area. Both the states and

Administrative areas are headed by the Governors and Chief Administrators respectively. As far as the chain of communication and line management is concerned, both the State governors and Area Chief Administrators are legitimately answerable to the President of the Republic.

Demographically, South Sudan remains a home to more than 11 million diverse inhabitants. However, other analysts place the exact figures to be more than the estimated 11 million people if the exact headcount could be transparently conducted nationwide. In terms of economic viability, South Sudan is one of the most impoverished countries in the world with 83 percent of its population living in rural and remote villages with poor communication and transport networks engulfed in acute poverty and widespread illiteracy. In this sense, the society of South Sudan is so dynamic culturally, geographically, and demographically, and whence does the nature of its education.

Ethnically, South Sudan is a multicultural and multi-religious nation-state with about sixty-four (64) tribes inhabiting the vast topographical territory of the most contemporary country. The inhabitants practice African traditional religions and communal beliefs, apparently practiced and contained mostly at the remote outside edge and local cities. Despite the modernization and civilization intact, most of the intellectuals, political leaders, and business elites, nonetheless, believe in witchcraft and cultural charms which are practiced widely across different communities. With common beliefs and hopes that once they are performed, they can improve one's prospects of employment and economic prosperity amongst other things.

As per the conventional wisdom and social expectations, hopes and expectations among the ordinary citizens of South Sudan remained high, at the time of independence. In line with the goals of the referendum, people were expecting their government to deliver the basic services including provision of quality educational opportunities, as well as taking towns closer to the people. To no avail, many basic necessities were not noticeably met, and so successive refractory civil wars and tribal conflicts tend to be the order of the day. For this reason, millions of lives have been lost, property destroyed and millions of people having been externally and internally displaced. Nevertheless, this implies that their leaders on both sides of the conflict have betrayed the fundamental rights of the people.

The socio-economic expectations and demands of the ordinary citizens were fully unmet, however, the rebellions and tribal conflicts started to emerge along ethnic lines. Some politicians and military leaders who felt their expectations were not fully accommodated, decided to rebel against the country's leadership system even before the independence of the country from the old Sudan. From an economic standpoint, South Sudan's national economy has been experiencing an economic meltdown following the outbreak of the South Sudanese civil wars since 2013 to date. The political differences have complicated equal participation of the communities in socio-economic domains and geo-political affairs. Hence, domestic market forces have widely been controlled by aliens and far-off mercenaries. However, the majority of the ordinary South Sudanese citizens are killing themselves over tribally affiliated leadership. This factor typically adds an insult to the already ailing national economy.

By virtue, all South Sudanese citizens deserve equitable rights to fully participate in the political and socio-economic spheres of life. The equal participation of diverse ethnic groups in the socio-economic and geo-political development should be inclusive and participatory in nature. However, this chipping in of diverse communities should be pro-active irrespective of political and religious affiliations, ethnic and racial compositions, geographic and demographic boundaries. This is an inevitable fact that everyone from any community or region should perceive and appreciate the importance of education. In this respect, South Sudanese communities may continue to maintain an inclusive approach to realize the continuity of learning during crises.

The prevailing point of view tends to support building a strong nation-state that is all-inclusive and ethnically represented. In this respect, Jok (2011) has maintained that nation-building is just not providing physical reconstruction, services, material prosperity, but employing the shared customs of the country so as to avoid potential conflict. In light of this, it suggests a nation that upholds societal values tend to collectively embrace for the national and cultural identities to prevail which may add weight to literacy boost in the face of crisis. I draw upon this practical idea from Prof. Jok in his emphasis on the central element to share established customs of all the communities without distinction. On this basis, respect of personal freedom and dignity should be within the context of the socio-economic comfort zone of the diverse communities.

In the interest of establishing a democratic nation, Jok's argument is logically sounding since social fabrics and communal structures among the South Sudanese people have been politically dejected and culturally weakened. This happened as a result of a lack of sharing common societal values and respecting common cultural identities. By means of inadequate political will among the South Sudanese leaders to accommodate the national norms and to treat them at an equal term and respect, most of the ethnic groups have become distrustful. Henceforth, tribal conflicts and hatred have ensued unexpectedly and uncontrollably.

Linking this reality to the importance of education, it may be mentioned that schooling is an elusive concept, which can be used to transform and shape the mindsets of the different ethnic communities especially at the grassroots levels. In his remarks, Jok upholds that spreading literacy into the village levels will enable many people to cherish positive cultural practices.

Henceforth, abandoning the archaic cultural practices which are harmful to one's life. Such destructive cultural practices like 'marking of foreheads' and the 'removal of lower teeth' in some South Sudanese communities have negative cultural implications to education.

While popular opinions may suggest aligning our collective egocentric ideals on equal treatment and respect of all people, I tend to support this idea earnestly. However, bringing into line such varied philosophies requires inclusive and particular approaches in terms of equal distribution of political, economic, and social necessities for all. This also requires fighting legally some harmful cultures that seem detrimental to our lives in general and to our education system particularly. In fact, most of the victims during the war range from communities, where some parts of their bodies have been marked as an indication of cultural prestige to signify symbolic heritage. This simply classifies some members of the community during the political tension and conflicts because they are culturally identified and eliminated by the warring forces.

On a different note, given the fact that South Sudan has a lower educational rate, it is imperative to note that providing mobile schooling to the nomadic communities has multifaceted benefits to pastoralists. In the first place, it will create a clear and modern transitional learning process from herding cattle to adopting modern and civility where ordinary citizens are engaged in non-violent activities. Secondly, furthering pastoral education countrywide may substantially transform and shape community lives to be civilized, constructive, and productive workforce. This may also add greater weight to national economic growth and individual civilization in a technologically-driven fashion and educationally sustainable environment.

However, this does not mean pastoral communities do not have civility and respect, but some of their cultural beliefs are sometimes self-contradictory to the security of other communities and international legal instruments. As an illustration, some of the nomadic communities that practice unhealthy cultural practices seem to be hostile compared to those communities which do not keep livestock in large quantities. In my view, the targeted killing of innocent civilians on the basis of tribal rivalries does not make a person or group of people to succeed the war. This is a different motive of tribal tendencies altogether during war and peacetime in South Sudan in particular and other war-affected regions in general.

The Political Context

As far as the political struggle within the leadership of the Sudan People's Liberation Movement (SPLM) is concerned, the political interests of the principal leaders overrode the social, economic, and cultural aspects of the ordinary people. As a case in point, the bloody competition of 2013 civil war was engineered by the party-political lobby on who should be the next SPLM Party's bearer to run for 2015 general elections as presidential candidate. Since it was not unsolved, the political and perceptive antagonism between the principal leaders led to the outbreak of 2013 civil war. This however, has led to the subsequent civil and political unrest which considerably expanded to the rest of the country. Henceforth, it brutally led to the loss of lives and destruction of property, on both sides of the conflict.

In December 2013, after president Salva Kiir accused opposition leader Riek Machar of attempting a coup, violent conflict broke out between government forces of the SPLM/A and anti-governmental groups. As a result of the political misunderstanding, the conflict quickly turned into a full-scale civil war spewed in mid-December 2013 in Juba pitting the forces of the government under President Salva Kiir Mayardit against the forces of the former Vice-President, Dr Riek Machar Teny. With

Map of the Republic of South Sudan depicting the Ten States and Three Administrative Areas

the ongoing civil war, many critics quickly concluded that the nature of the civil war took tribal and ethnic dimensions across South Sudan.

Hence, many civilians were taken hostage by tribal and ethnic forces with tens of thousands of people were subjected to untold suffering and political agony. It is significant to note that the war put a devastating toll on ordinary citizens particularly in deepening the economic hardships; thousands of lives were lost, millions of people were displaced internally and externally. Furthermore, untold destruction of the physical infrastructure of the government including educational facilities, private sectors, and the local and international organizations and agencies have witnessed the terrible part of human and material destruction countrywide.

In addition, several other political and communal militias joined the conflict from different war fronts. The political conflict quickly turned out to be a full-scale civil war and the peace negotiations between the two parties ensued. As much as peace is therefore concerned, a number of roundtable cease-fire attempts have been made in Addis Ababa, the Ethiopian Capital, brokered by the Inter-Governmental Authority on Drought (IGAD) to salvage the large-scale conflict. In 2015, the Agreement on the Resolution of the Conflict in South Sudan (ARCSS) was signed under the overall supervision of IGAD. However, both sides of the party signed with reservations, consequently, leading to a low profile of implementation. Mistrust among the 64 tribes shot up drastically even before the independence of South Sudan from the old Sudan.

It is imperative that the civil war that broke out in December 2013 was a result of a power struggle between the political elite who manipulated ethnic divisions and socio-economic grievances. Though the new unity government was set up to combat the violence, but it has done little to end the human rights abuses and improve the education system in the country. As a result of a lack of political will between the warring parties, and specifically the political leaders, peace collapsed, and this led to the fierce fighting in July 2016, in Juba. Afterwards, conflict quickly spread to the Equatoria and Upper Nile regions and some parts of Bahr el Ghazal. This characteristically led to massive displacement of civil populations and schools, especially in the war-affected states. In politically inspired violence, economic hardships were heavily felt within and outside the country in terms of inflation of local exchange rates against the hard currencies. This substantially increased the prices of essential and non-essential commodities in the local markets, henceforward complicating the living standards of ordinary citizens.

In spite of that, in 2018, both parties reached another peace agreement in the Sudanese capital, Khartoum, known as Khartoum Peace Agreement (KPA), brokered by the former Sudanese President Omer Hassan Al Bashir and was witnessed by the regional leaders. In the successive stages of peace negotiations, it turned out to be the revitalization of the ARCSS which came to known as the Revitalized Agreement on the Resolution of Conflict in South Sudan (R-ARCSS). Though it was received with joy by some South Sudanese population, doubts still lingered in the minds of the masses whether peace would be implementable and sustainable. This clearly manifested itself in the course of peace implementation which competing accusations and counteraccusations have been the order of the day.

On August 4th, 2021, Gen. Simon Gatwech Dual issued a communiqué for the removal of Dr Riek Machar following a meeting of opposition commanders at Kitgwang in Magenis, a northern-most town bordering Sudan. As a result, he declared himself as the leader of the SPLM-IO and that he has assumed power as the new opposition leader. He was backed up by Gen. Johnson Oliny, another militia commander of Agwelek forces stationed in north of the Upper Nile state. The Kitgwang SPLM/A-IO faction group pointed to a lack of trust, deviation of leadership direction and lack of political will from Dr Riek Machar, the SPLM/A-IO principal leader. On the other hand, Machar responded with another communiqué following a meeting of the SPLM-IO Political Bureau in Juba, the capital of South Sudan, and then accused unnamed "peace spoilers" of engineering the opposition split.

It should be mentioned that, since 2015, Gen. Simon Gatwech Dual has been the military Chief of General Staff of the SPLM/SPLA-IO and grew hostile horns against Machar since the signing of the revitalized peace agreement in 2018. For the interest of peace and stability, the government initiated another peace deal with the SPLM/A-IO breakaway Kitgwang faction group which was signed in Khartoum in January 2022. The peace agreement also guarantees the implementation of the security arrangements, a permanent ceasefire, grants the Kitgwang faction amnesty, establishment of cantonment sites, and reintegration of the breakaway SPLA-IO forces into the SSPDF within three months among others.

Mundy and Sarah (2011) have pointed out that, in the past

centuries, war and conflict may occur largely within rather than between nations as fighting happens within communities and involves ordinary civilians, spilling into homes, workplaces, and even schools. Absolutely, this is similar to what has been happening in South Sudan as a result of the South Sudanese Civil War which quickly spread from the capital Juba to the remote community levels. Henceforth, creating tensions and sectional confrontations that are viewed by some political analysts to be turning into a genocidal war, if not handled adequately. Indeed, ethnically targeted killings became the order of the day in Juba, state levels, and also on the major highways leading in and outside of Juba. It should be noted that this is a cheap and empty politics that has so far been pitting the South Sudan communities against themselves.

In fact, targeting and slaughtering vulnerable civilians represents significant war crimes and crimes against humanity, according to the statute of Hague-based International Criminal Court (ICC). In military practice of war, civilians and vulnerable groups are known as non-combatants, and they should not be targeted by any armed skirmishes on both sides of the conflict. In my viewpoint, destruction and occupation of school facilities by armed groups has been at a minimal deadlock. However, if school occupation or destruction is squarely done on purpose or by accident, it legally amounts to huge chastisement to a large extent. On this account, such annihilations of learning facilities disown the national educational goals at the expense of the ordinary citizens.

Worse still, most of the ethnic groupings have been involved in promoting varied hate speech on different media platforms and social forums. As a result, these have rotationally created an indigenous disenfranchisement and some degrees of participation in the socio-economic development. Likewise, ethnic groups have developed a strong hatred which has led to social and political discrimination, tribalism, job discrimination and geopolitical segregation. Undeniably, they are in fact used as alternative weapons of war by supporters of principal parties including independent and interests-based groups. In fact, such discriminatory behaviors have consistently fueled and prolonged the armed conflicts and intercommunal skirmishes across South Sudan. In addition, a lack of formal military training accentuates that majority of armed groups have failed to effectively control and command their forces. Tangibly, this has inflicted an untold suffering to the unarmed civil population.

In purely combat terms, armed leaders should take into consideration the Rules of Engagement (RoE) that guide their operations to protect ordinary citizens and their property. This should also be supplemented by the *'Do No Harm Policy'* in the context of military operations during the wars. However, this has not been the case in the context of South Sudanese waged conflicts. In multiple fronts, any civilian announces his or her intentional rebellion without having gone under military training including his or her militants. As a result of ill-manners or no training at all, such leaders have always led massive destruction to civilians such as looting. This singlehandedly resulted into the killing of civilians, maiming of children and scarcely failing to effectively command and control their respective forces.

On the other hand, most of the rebel field commanders in South Sudan lack adequate formal military training on command duties and staff leadership. They lack strong political and economic manifestos for military operations to strictly observe rules of engagements in their respective controlled territories. On the odd occasion, one may develop contradictory feelings about adversary forces in terms of military destructive behaviors of not allowing access to humanitarian activities. This factual circumstance points to the reality that the objectives of the war, are conceivably, geared towards building tribal agenda rather than advancing national and patriotic objectives. Such discrimination against other members living in one's operational area of jurisdiction, is an indication of a lack of effective civil-military relations between the army leadership and the civil populations. On that account, trust and combined efforts between the army and the civilian population have totally been lost, given their patriotic connotation and objective approaches of war.

The Emergency Context

The typical way of thinking about education during emergencies has some connections with a history of conflicts and naturally occurring phenomena. To a larger extent, such devastating events or disasters detrimentally affect the lives of ordinary citizens and the destruction of their physical facilities. It is worth mentioning that some negative impacts may occur in varying degrees at different times and places. The climax of the crisis in genuine sense believes education as a wide-reaching issue of overriding concern. However, it has been neglected and undermined by some countries during the emergency and non-emergency contexts.

In all conflict situations, the key reasons for unsafe and inaccessible learning spaces are a result of increased demand from internally displaced persons and refugees. This is also tracked by destruction caused by conflict and other disreputable hazards. In addition, the occupation and use of schools by IDPs, refugees, the military or armed groups have gained negative impressions on the continuity of learning. This requires lifelike interventions to address this issue, though the reproach varies because of the different contexts and related reasons for that matter.

The situation in South Sudan is still unstable with frequent reports on civil unrest resulting from continued communal revenge wars in a number of villages and counties. Moreover, cattle raids and criminal activities on the roads have aggravated the already ailing socio-economic and political crises. There are now out-of-the-way accounts of the occupation of schools by warring armies. In this essence, floods have destroyed school structures and displaced populations, hereafter confining them to camps or neighboring countries. The displaced populations are unable to farm the land, which basically exacerbate the level of food insecurity and poverty. Some children have stopped attending school due to a lack of school fees and essential needs to support their schooling.

The impact of conflict and closure of schools for more than a year due to the COVID-19 pandemic, has kept some learners including teachers away from the learning centers. Most significantly, countries of the world have suffered such calamities, and South Sudan is amongst them. On a similar vein, teacher crisis is at the heart of the global learning predicament. There is a universal shortage of motivated and well-trained teachers, and South Sudan profoundly suffers from this problem. Emergency has made it very hard to acquire a qualified teaching force to provide the quality teaching and learning activities required for boys and girls to succeed throughout their professional and career pathways.

By the same token, independent scholars and governments have interchangeably used emergency to refer to the crisis. In the event of the happening of crises, different scholars, government bureaucracies, and multilayered humanitarian and development agencies have quickly referred crises as emergencies. In spite of that, the definition of emergency remains a debatable term in the contemporary world. As a result, there is no standard accepted definition of emergency, which has been agreed upon by different scholars and academics. However, this implies that an emergency is a wide and new concept defined differently by different scholars for different situations.

Notwithstanding, the different definitions attached to the word emergency, can be the result of natural and man-made activities. In simple terms, natural emergencies are those that occur in the predictable environment such as floods, typhoons, thunderstorms, bush fire, et cetera. On the other hand, man-made emergencies are those created by human beings such as wars, intra-sectional and inter-communal conflicts, just to mention a few. In a coherent definition, conflict is typically defined as any situation in which an armed violence emerges within the government or among the communities and disrupts the lives and livelihood of citizens. Nonetheless, both emergencies have negative implications on the lives of human beings and their property.

My simple conventional conviction is that much of the occurring emergencies are a result of human manipulative happenings, which have consequential effects on their socio-economic activities. As a result of these man-made calamities and inevitable catastrophes, both economic, political and social structures, to a larger extent, are negatively affected. However, the education sector is more affected than other sectors. This is because education is one of the most important sectors where human beings place more highbrow emphasis and prospective hopes due to various socio-economic benefits. It is the sector to which educational knowledge can be used to transform societal values and improve economic growth to keep the check and balance of socioeconomic progress for sustainable societies. Principally, by knowledge of education, this can realize the socio-economic development and technological progress of the communities, which currently constitute the Republic of South Sudan.

By far and large, EiE represents a significant field within the wider spectrum of learning and teaching domains. It is being treated as a vibrant tool to be used during an emergency context to maintain the continuity of learning and so as to complete a given educational cycle. It has been gaining mutual recognition in some parts of the world as a viable affirmative action to intervene and salvage man-made and natural disasters in the respective distressed communities. Practically, when it comes to the provision of education during crises, this has been given low attention by both the donor communities and the governments of the fragile member-states. According to the Department of Foreign and International Development (DFID), fragile states are those where the government cannot or will not deliver core functions to the majority of its citizens, including the poor and the marginalized groups. This leads us to define fragility, as the state where a country falls to provide basic services to poor people because they are unwilling to do so because of lack of political will and legal commitment.

As far as educational resources are affected either directly or indirectly, this book explores further the undesirable impacts of armed conflict and other naturally occurring phenomena on education, particularly in emergency situations. Because of a number of large-scale civil wars waged in South Sudan by different insurgent groups, before and after independence, successive educational systems have been affected negatively to underperform. Not only that, but the manpower and physical infrastructures have been deliberately affected and physically shattered in the eyes of the principal leaders and their supporting hegemonic groups.

It is a visible indicator in South Sudan where some schools, teaching forces, students, and parents are often targeted by the armed forces. For instance, students and teachers are vulnerable to recruitment into the armed forces, either willingly or unwillingly. At some points, schools are occupied by the armed forces, and this leads to the displacement of teachers, learners and parents. On the other hand, girls continue to be the major targets due to specific discrimination as coupled with their position of vulnerabilities in the receptive societies. In more obvious cases, girls have been subjected to rape, sexual assault, sexual harassment, arbitrarily abduction, and forced marriage being differentiated against them on the basis of gender.

By operational definition, Cahill (2010) defines Emergency as *"any crisis situation, arising from natural causes to armed conflict, which may be international or internal, or post-conflict situations that impair, interrupt, delay, deny or impede the right to education."* To search for survival in an emergency perspective, real-world situations present themselves devastating in similar ways in which human beings are presumed to suffer. This typically points toward the reality that emergency situation will continue to succeed if human behaviors with regards to individual, political, and economic interests are not surpassed.

From my own practical interpretation of the term, the concept of emergency is any expected or unexpected state of crisis that is either triggered by man-made activities or natural calamities, which can affect both human lives and substantial assets. Put differently, emergency refers to an expected hostile situation that leads to the loss of human and material lives, either caused by human activities or occurring naturally in a given environment. In light of this dimensional characterization of emergency, it may be collectively mentioned that an emergency is both a natural and manmade phenomena. As a result, the magnitudes of emergency can be destructive and life-threatening in nature.

In the same way, Nicolai (2003) defined an emergency as any crisis that turns out to be overwhelming to the capacity of the community to cope up with the meager resources at their disposal. Without a doubt, emergency is largely experienced in conflict-affected states since they are overwhelmed in the natural phenomena. In this sense, Samman et al. (2018) define conflict-affected states to be those, which have fragile institutions and low capacities to deliver quality and fair policies, as well as being part of the problem in marginalizing the minorities. In this essence, this is true to the extent that some communities may be victimized in situations where laws of the land are not applied adequately because of fragile institutional capacities, political interference and economic influence. In light of this definition, it could be comprehended that emergency happens at anywhere in the world and both human and material resources are affected, though the degree and intensity of the calamities vary from one community to the other. Education-wise, emergencies continue to affect the schooling of the learners and the welfare of the teaching force. In this way, peace education is threatened, and learners in schools and the respective communities are traumatized in the process of executing political conflict by contestant forces.

In contemporary educational settings under the pretext of fragile states, two terms of education in emergencies and education in crises emerge substantially. Conversely, EiE and Education in crisis-affected contexts are used interchangeably to refer to the provision of educational practices and program interventions designed to help the communities affected by conflicts and other naturally occurring disasters (Burde, 2015). In my personal reflection on EiE, I view EiE as the application of educational resources, knowledge, skills, and expertise in an effort to address the hostile situations that are overpowering the learning institutions of the affected communities. This characteristically puts EiE to be defined as the provision of schooling in humanitarian emergencies caused by conflicts and wars, natural disasters, health and environmental related crises. Even now, other scholars concede that; EiE is the provision and continuity of educational opportunities during crises in a protective, supportive and inclusive learning environment.

As far as education in an emergency context is concerned, it should be mentioned that crises of all sorts have become rampant in the past and may present contradictory human history. In this view, the adversative impacts routinely affect the normalcy of the school community and the operationalization of its educational activities. Though the degree of damage and loss of property remain not always the same in all emergency contexts, it should be admitted that the consequences at some points become very devastating to human lives. Furthermore, it can be destructive to physical features and infrastructural facilities. According to Cahill (2010), such situations establish people's health and lives at risk and either threaten or destroy public and private assets at will. Henceforward, it limits the capacity and available resources to guarantee human rights to education and uphold social responsibilities.

In the context of South Sudan, naturally occurring disasters are exceedingly rare in some regions, but common in others. These include famine and floods, which normally happen at some distinct vicinities. This means that South Sudan is one of the blessed nations with extremely limited occurrences of natural disasters. However, most of the disasters and emergencies are human-triggered aspects such as civil wars, intra-communal and inter-communal conflicts, and others. In this context, it is precise to mention that such man-made catastrophes usually become so complex and tense when they strike unexpectedly. This virtuously translates into a dire situation, which is impending to the loss of millions of lives and destruction of property.

Viewing it from an angle of school set-ups, it should be mentioned that most of the fascinating learning and teaching activities have been disrupted either partially or completely in some parts of the country as a result of conflict crises. In point of fact, most of the administrative and teaching programs of the affected schools have been brought to a standstill. In fact, it should be distinguished that non-participation of the community in educational affairs has widened the political and social gaps among members of diverse ethnic backgrounds. This practice is, in fact, corroborated by wrong perceptions as attributed to a lack of cooperation and collaboration among different ethnic groups. In this context, it has formed some negative sensitivities and sectional perceptions that encourage the spread of hate speech by some South Sudanese communities against each other. For such reasons, the application of educational knowledge and skills, to address the crises remain the most effective tool to propel the country forward.

In this context, the most compelling case in point is the

learning institutions affected by the armed conflict in South Sudan include learning institutions in the Greater Upper Nile, Greater Equatoria and some parts of the Greater Bahr El Ghazal regions. In some parts of Equatoria, for instance, some schools in Eastern Equatoria State, former Central Equatoria, and Western Equatoria States have suffered a devastating blow in terms of massive displacement of people and teaching force. This is also coupled by a destruction of school infrastructures and the loss of innocent lives. Undistinguishably, another drawback is that some schools in Unity, Jonglei, and Upper Nile states have also witnessed similar destructions and fixed with internal and external displacement of citizens.

At the tertiary level, destruction of learning facilities and looting of educational resources either intentionally or unintentionally was used as a weapon of war. Amongst the affected tertiary institutions were the University of Upper Nile and Dr. John Garang Memorial University of Science and Technology. These universities were ransacked and completely vandalized by armed forces in the wake of the political crisis which pitted government forces against the rebel mutineers in 2013. As a result of the war, the University of Upper Nile had to be relocated to Juba after its operations were suspended for about 3 years due to cumulative insecurity and was coupled with a lack of a learning space.

In fact, most areas were profoundly affected by the conflict due to the presence of strong holds of the rebel and government forces which may lead to constant confrontations here and now. With regard to the continuous and perpetual conflicts, the suffering of the innocent citizens was at full gear in those respective conflict zones. As the saying goes, when elephants fight, it is the grass that suffers the most. This was exactly what happened as a result of successive civils wars which negatively affected the national education system. This is illustrated by Sommers (2004) that in terms of co-ordination, war-affected, displaced, disempowered, and traumatized communities are indisputably the grass. For me, this is demonstrated in the real-life situations that civil populations have suffered in the hands of both the rebel and government forces before and after the eruption of the 2013 and 2016 crises in Juba, respectively.

On that account, the crisis exposed average and innocent citizens to an act of brutality and destructive activities. As a matter of fact, most of civilians were exposed to isolated target killings carried out by unknown gunmen and gunwomen along the major highways, particularly those leading in and out of Juba. Though both the government and the rebel forces trade accusations and push the blame game on one another in relation to who committed such brutal acts to the civil entities, it is true that both committed crimes and crimes against humanity. Undeniably, both parties and other tribal leaders who play cold politics along the tribal dimensions have contributed to the disappearance of both human lives and the destruction of material resources. On a square basis, this negative approach to conflict enters one's mind when considering the nature of crimes being committed. These singlehandedly resulted to target killing of certain ethnicities in different states and regions, and also within the surrounding areas.

As emergencies continue in South Sudan, educational personnel were reported dead in embattled assassinations in some parts of the country affected by the conflict. However, this is not new in man-made emergencies since ordinary citizens suffer adverse effects. This is true in a sense that citizens of certain areas are found to be supporting and collaborating with either the leadership of the rebels or the government. Notwithstanding, Cahill (2010) argues that when an emergency strikes, teachers, students, and parents become the targets of violence. As such, there are no clear statistics to prove the targeted killings of teachers and students in the South Sudanese conflict. However, target killings and massive displacement of teachers, students, and parents is a visible indicator of learning institutions being targeted during the conflict. In addition, there are still, no clear reports in South Sudan that prove whether educational facilities were intentionally or unintentionally destroyed by the armed forces on both sides of the conflict.

From the gender perspective, more boys, girls, and men were killed in the conflict. Indeed, ethnic hatred, oppression, and intolerance are common among women and girls. In most cases, fighting forces ordinarily use sexual violence as a weapon of war (Mundy & Sarah, 2011). Throughout the conflict, brutal and inhumane activities have been reported across South Sudan. This has been substantiated by different reports from different media outlets on death rates in the protracted South Sudanese conflicts. However, in this book, there are no accurate figures for the loss of lives since the reports have been negatively influenced by different reporters.

In fact, most of the journalists and intellectuals have taken a political and social side in the interpretation of the conflict, especially when it comes to personal accounts and reporting mechanisms. It could be observed that some journalists who either hail from Equatoria, Bahr el Ghazal, or Upper Nile Regions do not account accurately for what actually emerged on the grounds, as most reports and news headlines are often exaggerated. At some points reports of killings and intimidations are edited by tribally-aligned journalists and scholars to fit their personal interests and dogmatic gains in support of a given political agenda and locality.

On the other hand, girl education is of course, affected in the conflict-prone nations including South Sudan. It is imperative to point out that female education in South Sudan, in particular, has been detrimentally affected by the conflict due to the fact that the implementation of the existing policy for girl education has not been effectively materialized. In fact, most girls feel unsafe whenever insecurity is observable in different conflict zones. Yet, it could be argued that despite the already prevailing cultural traditions which hinder girls from benefiting right education. Indeed, this is worsened by poor delivery of educational activities and needs-based content in the hostile school environment, which itself, is life-threatening and discriminatory in the approach.

Generally, girl education even during non-emergency situations is not given immediate thoughtfulness in South Sudan and other war-affected regions around the globe. As it happens, negative attitudes of parents towards girl education resurface and complicate girl child education not only during emergency situations but also during non-emergency contexts. Despite these materiality, both parties to the conflict have carried out tribally supported killing and rapes during the war times especially in the isolated peripheries, which has very much affected girl education. Indeed, the fact dwells that the Statutes of the International Criminal Court (ICC) Article recognizes rape and other gender-based violence as a specific war crime and crimes against humanity. According to Mundy and Sarah (2011), the peace agreements signed recognize rape and other forms of sexual violence and attacks, but many women and girls still experience gender-based violence including traditional practices.

Certainly, customary practices such as forced marriage, ignorance of girl education, and domestic violence top the list of gender discrimination in the corresponding communities in South Sudan. This is also coupled with a lack of adequate sanitation facilities that hinder the will of pubescent to stay at home. Most girls on their monthly period need privacy, in consequence, most of the schools in the context of South Sudan lack these disaggregated change rooms for female learners. In this context, the Landmark UN Security Council Resolution on Women, Peace, and Security (UNSCR, 1325) (United Nations Security Council, 2000) recognizes the need to protect women and girls from sexual violence. With specific attention to the particular protection and participation of girls, UNSCR 1325 can provide an extremely useful policy framework like gender equality in education in times of crisis. In this note, fragile states can provide specific activities for women such as tailoring, capital, health services, training and education in an effort to bring peace and security.

In spite of that, this antagonistic situation in South Sudan has already led to the massive loss of innocent lives and destruction of property as a result of continuous wars and tribal sentiments. In a similar fashion, it has led to the destruction of communal social fabrics and societal configurations of different ethnic groups have been exposed to a desperately critical outlook. On that account, such situations have already created fertile grounds for disagreement, tribalism, segregation, sectarianism, and mistrust among the South Sudanese communities, both in and outside the country. In order to find a wave of lasting peace and trusting relationships, it is critical for the government and its educational actors to recognize and support education in the face of crises. As such, this requires magnifying more robust approaches, collective efforts and devise rapid response strategies to be applied in the times of crisis. By doing so, this is primarily aimed at providing and guaranteeing a conducive learning atmosphere for all learners and educational work force in a non-threatening environment.

The Educational Context

South Sudan, like any other country in the world, has its own structured national Education System. The system of Education has been designed with a tremendous task to transmit educational goals to shape societal values and improves one's prospects of living. For some reasons, the South Sudan education system has been performing under certain conditions both in the pre-transition and post-independence periods. The two

The Author (in Red jacket) with some pastoralist youth in Abalek cattle campsite in Malual-Muok section, Tonj South County, Warrap State (Courtesy of 2019)

consecutive periods have not put much focus and emphasis on the national education system in terms of educational relevance and sustainability of life skills.

At the same time, adaptive learning measures are not practically taken into account in the manner that can reshape the political, economic, social, cultural, scientific, and philosophical features of a transformed society. In this way, such transformations and modernizations of societal values and well-being may not happen out of the blue, but through redirecting the relevant education system that answers community complications. Virtually, the relevancy of education can carry out a crucial role in responding community needs both during the emergency and in the post-conflict reconstructions.

Typical sense seems to visualize the fact that ordinary citizens have echoed their concerns regarding the components of learning in the national Education System of South Sudan as being contextually irrelevant. Based on varying opinions from different stakeholders and clients, the current system of education has immense teaching and learning goals, which do not actually produce quality education as expected by the ordinary citizens. This implies that the teaching and learning processes at all levels of education do not encourage creative and innovative approaches in light of the acquisition of quality and relevant educational knowledge. In this respect, knowledge acquisition is one thing, and knowledge construction and application of relevant job skills in the practical realities of life is another thing. The distinguished conventional wisdom of the importance of schooling tells us that education has always been considered a vital tool for developing human and material resources during emergency a nd non-emergency contexts.

As a case in point, EiE remains a viable element that can supplement the educational activities in shaping human capacity and mitigating conflict in the face of crises. The practical implication is that education could possibly be provided anywhere and at any time with or without crises so as to keep the learning in an exciting continuity. Of course, it points to the fact that education as a means for transmitting knowledge and skills to the learners is basically considered to be one of the key components of peace of mind and should be provided alongside the humanitarian services and development undertakings. In pursuit of EiE during crises, Education Cannot Wait (ECW Strategy 2018-2021) has specifically stressed that all learners including boys and girls may be exposed to danger such as sexual exploitation, conscription into the armed forces or injured during the crises. On this ground, there are many striking instances of child exploitation in alternative forms as a result of conflicts and wars, ranging here and now. In relative terms, it is understandable that all types of emergencies detrimentally affect learning institutions. Factually, this shows that emergency situations of any form affect the smooth running of the school activities including the community neighborhood.

From the lens of female education, the central rhetorical move is that girls remain the frontier victims due to the specific judgments related to discriminatory cultural factors. As such, the possibility of extending girl child education goes on to be critical as endless wars and ethnic tensions become the order of the day in this twentieth-first century. In practical realities, girls continue to be victimized by both their parents and the armed forces due to their weaker positions engineered by specifically defined gender roles in different societies. To a larger extent, an important point to take note is that girls become victims of rape, forced marriage, sexual abuse as well as being isolated from educational settings. Largely, this alone undermines the rights of girls to engage in their educational aspirations to realize professional development and economic dependency.

On the other hand, schools are disserted by the teaching force as a result of the forced recruitment of teachers and support staff. In fact, most of the qualified teachers have been abandoning the teaching job since then, because of the fact that the teaching profession in South Sudan has been faced with a lot of challenges such as lack of motivation, low payment and inadequate professional development, just to mention a few. From a unique angle, such deep motivations have created low morale among the teaching force to commit to the teaching profession during crises. Nevertheless, there have been many persistent problems even before the crises. As a result, most of the teachers have nowadays developed low morale in their teaching profession.

Given this background, the majority of the teaching force has abandoned their duty stations either voluntarily in search of other green pastures outside their noble profession. Surprisingly, the students being admitted to the teaching profession do not choose education programs on the basis of their professional aspirations. However, some may reject their educational courses once they are admitted to the public universities with the justifications that education is a poor profession financially and morally. This relates to the fact that they consider it a poor university course that makes them become poorer when they complete their professional program of study. However, this is not true in the sense that no university program is a bad course. The tendency of being a bad or good one depends on the curiosity of the student on his or her professional aspirations and commitment to study.

Despite the efforts exerted by domestic governments and humanitarian actors to address the emerging crises, basic needs and expectations remain very high among the affected populace. In light of these educational controversies, Smith (2009) argues that education can be derailed back due to a lack of political will by the central government to prioritize educational activities especially in areas of funding and equitable distribution of educational resources and programs. Although I concede this, I still maintain that education is hugely affected by a lack of political spaces. Persistence of a limited political space will affect the educational activities in the face of crises.

Equally important, EiE can offer unique windows of opportunities to build the capacities of the teaching force in the areas of teaching, administration and school leadership so as to cope up with unfriendly situations. Fundamentally, EiE stresses the need to provide pre-service and in-service training opportunities to teachers so that they are able to support, monitor, assess, supervise, and evaluate the learning and teaching activities. As far as building democratic and vibrant societies through education is very much concerned, EiE is well-thought-of to be an effective contrivance that needs to be applied in order to enhance peacebuilding and conflict mitigation. Though the application of quality and similar educational opportunities are of the limited stream, educational access remains an obstacle that requires shared efforts.

In this setting, affirmative educational interventions may also include DRR that encourages the continuity of learning.

This may restore trust and confidence among the people in a manner that encourages democratic and useful processes. Put differently, EiE can help to minimize the dropout of girls due to forced marriages, early pregnancies, as well as protecting the learners and their learning spaces. Conversely, it could be mentioned that both the humanitarian actors and donor agencies largely ignore education during emergencies. Yet, much more attention is only given to humanitarian support in the form of food and medical supplies. From the humanitarian perspective, this creates social inequality in terms of the delivery of basic services during crises.

Finally, this book underscores the roles of the coordination and partnerships of educational programs and activities that could collectively be carried out by the government, humanitarian and education policy actors, donor communities, the leadership of schools and the wider community members. In this line of thinking, the overriding paradigm of EiE is that lack of implementation of education policy during crises remains a major challenge facing the country by the time of writing this book. It is important to notice that the education system of South Sudan has neither been popularized nor implemented in the letter and spirit. Wholly, the directives in relation to national educational aims are decided by the political and economic elites of the country. This political discourse limits the universality of the education system in South Sudan. For this reason, it is being treated as the concept of the central system decided from a top-down leadership approach.

Apparently, the South Sudan education system is being treated as a self-insufficient system in its very nature. In fact, it is being regarded as a very significant subsystem of a total shared system, which casts a lot of things to be desired. I call it a subsystem of an intact social system because it has been underperforming and much of its educational and curriculum goals are not aligned principally to meet the community expectations up to this point in time. Yet, ordinary citizens are so enthusiastic to strategize and maximize the rather educational standards they want in order to realize the national educational goals that can transform the communities during the emergency and non-emergency contexts. Being contextually irrelevant, the system is made vulnerable to be influenced either directly or indirectly by the political elites of the country.

On this account, educational inputs, performance, and output of the country's leadership and the outside world will continue to perform poorly. As such, all levels of education are restrained by the government in terms of availing appropriate curriculum and effective school administration. As a result, there is no guarantee of uniformity from one region to another in terms of quality educational standards expected out of the national education system per se. This socio-economic state in the context of the education system derails the spirit of pulling together the effective education system that resolves the obvious problems of all the communities during political predicaments.

Undeniably, failure to provide such learning opportunities remains a threat to national security. This may derail peaceful settlements among themselves and the host communities due to heightening tribal conflicts across the country. I have always believed that most of the nomadic communities are not enlightened and sensitized about the importance of education and peaceful coexistence among themselves and with their hosts. Since the government is the sole provider of basic services, my view is that; the nomadic communities should have equal right to basic education. If pastoralist communities are inconsiderately neglected in the education system, this noticeably suggests that they are socially, culturally, economically, and professionally disconnected from the rest of the societies. In reality, an all-inclusive education approach that considers pastoral education as an alternative means to reduce illiteracy in the country could be the best way forward.

On the positive part, education distinctively contributes to the acquisition of beneficial social impact at individual and community levels and from all spheres of life. In this sense, I am convinced that advancing a competency-based curriculum that provides equal educational prospects for all offer the only viable solution to be given due attention. Equally important, pastoral education initiatives can be communicated across cultural lines with more focus on the independent-mindedness of the nomadic youths to attain quality education. Essentially, this may meet the reality of a culturally responsive curriculum that respects and acknowledges the cultures of the nomadic communities and not to be contradictory with the national and above-board laws.

On the other hand, advancing basic educational services in rural settings in form of mobile schooling is more perceptible than reforming the education agenda. This substantially can add a heavyweight to the attainment of literacy and numeracy goals at the national level. It is equally important to observe that pastoral education is a feasible alternative to disseminate the true meaning of the intellectual capital to the mindsets of the youth by enabling them to access knowledge and skills to become productive and peace-loving citizens. In so doing will heighten the educational reality that the more they are educated the more they can access vital key messages and life-sustaining information for survival and safety purposes. Though the functioning of the school-based learning approach is universally accepted to a larger extent, the mainstream education system is still weak. I still maintain that it largely ignores the mobile schooling strategy that can be applied to engage nomadic communities actively and constructively.

In purely an inclusive term, education should be made accessible, affordable, and even-handed based on a non-discriminatory approach for all. From a security-wise perspective, pastoral education could also add a practical advantage to the improvement and submission to national security laws that safeguard the country. Undeniably, failure to provide such learning opportunities will continue to be another threat to national security and may continue derailing peaceful settlements among themselves and the host communities due to heightening tribal conflicts. In my personal perspective, leaving out the pastoralists in the education system will continue to be a true-life threat to national economic development since most of them do not go by the law. However, keeping them in the school settings within their socio-economic vicinity will minimize cattle raiding and thefts of different forms.

On a different note, providing mobile schooling to the nomadic communities will develop a direct pathway to the modern transitional learning process from herding cattle in a non-violent approach. By furthering pastoral education, it may be admitted that educational outcomes as a result of these activities will substantially transform and shape community lives to be a more civilized, constructive, and productive workforce that adds weight to national economic growth in a technologically driven fashion. Personally, I believe that leaving out the pastoralists in the education system will continue to be a true-life threat to the national economy since most of them do not go by the law. However, keeping them in the school settings within their vicinity will minimize cattle raiding and thefts for instance.

The prevailing point of view is that continuing the learning perspectives may increase the acquisition of talents from the school during war times. The talents remain underutilized, and this may contribute to positive coexistence between the rebels on the one hand, and the government on the other hand. Providing the youths with soft and life skills is substantially recycled and constructively appraised for the common good of mankind in some given geographic entities. In the same way, EiE can play some crucial roles expressly in the promotion of social and political equality among the different ethnic groups.

This could happen in the pretext that youths are prepared to be responsible and resourceful citizens in different political, social, cultural, and economic spheres of life.

Forthrightly speaking, most existing educational infrastructures in South Sudan and particularly in the most war-affected regions are constructed using the funds from education partners and stakeholders. As such, I am convinced that providing educational opportunities during emergencies is a critical milestone to enhance educational enfranchisement and economic development. In fact, education capacitates human resource development that can shape the education systems as well as foster individual and intellectual growth. Though the government and other education actors at unique socio-economic angles frequently overlook education as an ultimate goal. In spite of that, the fact dwells that education is actually the best way forward for peacebuilding and conflict mitigation. Similarly, education leads to conflict moderation, skills improvement, and capacity building in broader social and economic contexts. Indeed, placing a considerable emphasis on education in emergencies constitutes the major starting point for the critical realization of educational goals, both as long-term and short-term possible strategies.

During an emergency, the school environment is not always safe, and providing a protected learning space is the most significant outcome during crises. To provide school safety and security, the school leadership and the government should provide ultimate and maximum custody to protect the learners, teachers, non-teaching support staff, and the school property. Daniels and Brandley (2011) suggest there are characteristics of the social-emotional climate that relate to school safety such as skills instruction, expected student behavior, engagement with the community, student awareness and positive adult awareness. In this spirit, conventional wisdom indicates that social-emotional development among the learners and the school personnel remains an integral part to be considered during an emergency context.

On a different note, in a school environment where ethnic tensions and divisions are gaining momentum, it is imperative that school leadership besides the government should continue to build and encourage beneficial adult interactions within and outside the school environment. Daniels and Branley (2011) underscored that positive adult interactions include adults displaying warmth and interest, behaving as positive role models of authority figures, and engaging prejudiced treatment for all students. Indeed, establishing trusting relationships among the learners and the teaching breaks the code of silence, consequently maintaining equal treatment for all people with dignity and respect of all forms.

With the building of positive adult interaction in the school environment, both the students, teachers, and the broader community around the school feel safe as their children's rights and dignities are being given due respect and consideration. As such, it is an obligatory role for the teachers, parents, and the government to build and encourage positive adult interactions among students from different communities, with diverse ethnic backgrounds and social compositions. As far as EiE is theoretically and practically concerned, two things are critical: ethnic division and demographic isolation in the context of South Sudan.

From this impression, it is obvious that South Sudanese communities have been alienated along ethnic lines, as a consequence, it may create unfavorable social and political networks not only among their peers but also in the wider learning environment. In light of this, education in emergencies brings people together to better acknowledge and foster human connections and transparent relationships with students from all works of life. However, this does not come out of the blue, but it involves a high level of transparency to be catered to along with the provision of emotional and social protection. Primarily, such level of commitment and transparency of the leaders is to encourage respect for cultural diversity among learners, teachers and parents in their social and cultural settings. This makes the adaptation to respond to different needs as insecurity continues to intensify. On this line, what is more, important is the variation to teach the child in a protective and supportive learning environment.

PART TWO
The Importance of Education in the Times of Crises

Education as a Safe Sanctuary for Learners and the School Personnel

Appropriate education under no circumstances, is the most important thing in our personal lives. It is a continuous and lifelong process to be obtained through the organized learning, training and research. It brings important changes in our lives through socio-economic prosperity and meaningful human resource development. By and large, education is the foundation of human development and technological growth. Essentially, a good education merely gives everyone to typically grow and succeed regardless of all odds of social life. Ideally, education is important to men and women as both have indispensable roles in the development of a heathy and sustainable society. Despite any type of emergency, education continues to be an exciting tool to transform devastated human lives, restore trust and inspire peaceful coexistence to the affected communities.

During an emergency context, education is significantly considered as an alternative to keep children and young adults safe, active and alive. This is because learning institutions are properly protected when they are functioning, but are likely to be occupied by the armed forces when they are non-functional. This basically demands the government and other education actors to keep the schools secure, safe and functional in the face of crises. On this basis, during crises and emergency situations, schools become safe havens for protecting learners, youths, teachers, and the surrounding members of the school community. In the same way, schools provide some sort of protection and capacity building to the members of the community through training events. In this way, the capacity building programs may include important seminars, workshops, and life-sustaining pieces of preparation in which shattered societies are socially rebuilt.

On a different lens, many people assume that the psychosocial and emotional effects of conflict do not easily pave the way until effective measures and interventions are employed to address the broad range of educational issues. For instance, these may include teachers' well-being, the maintenance of the school environment, and the protection of learners. For apparent reasons, many ordinary citizens are opposed to this idea, as most of them do not let their children go to school in the event that conflict is intensifying. This is at present a dreadful mistake for parents and guardians to keep children out of school during crises. Legitimately, some domestic and international laws protect schools from being occupied or destroyed by the opposing forces. In this way, letting the continuity of teaching and learning activities is counterproductive and should be highly emphasized and financially supported.

Though there are obvious shreds of evidence on the attacks of the school in the war-torn countries including South Sudan, it happens under certain violations of the Rules of Engagement (RoE) by the mutual parties to the conflicts. However, this is not directly done intentionally in a direct confrontation, but such activities are done meanderingly in isolation within the learning institutions, which could be categorized as acts of terrorism. In the school settings, attacks on school personnel and the occupation of schools legally constitute war crimes and crimes against humanity. In a similar line, Smith (2009) concedes that education offers protection and other support to the learners during emergencies, post-conflict as well as in the state of fragility. This implies that the utmost learning institutions are protected by the government including international and national organizations. Consequently, this makes it easy for the safety of the learners to be guaranteed and protected.

Education as a Catalyst for Peacebuilding and Conflict Mitigation

Peace is nothing other than the availability of freedom, justice, social transparency and access to learning opportunities. Likewise, it is about streamlining peaceful efforts which are geared toward conflict resolution and democratization of the administrative departments of the government. EiE has repeatedly been emphasized as the key factor for the investment of human resource development. Notably, it is believed that education can also mitigate conflict during encountered situations. As a worthwhile tool, education is managed to mitigate conflict in a variety of ways between the warring parties including the members of the society who might have lost trust and hope in the future and in their leaders as well. In this respect, Cahill (2010) enumerates that education promotes conflict resolution and peacebuilding, social cohesion, democratic tolerance, and respect for human rights.

From my standpoint, it is equally precise in the sense that education plays multiple roles in the reconstruction of post-conflict societies. This could be performed by bringing together the parties to the conflicts under one umbrella of peace and democratic principles to compromise their demands for the sake of peaceful coexistence and unity of the wider suffering population. It is within the context of providing education in an emergency context in which those awful social fabrics and shattered social structures are restructured once again in society. In this respect, the best needs of the people are met as sufficiently as respect for human rights and personal dignity is restored by the application of competent rule of law to realize fairer justice.

On the other hand, Culbertson and Constant (2015) believe that a school building strategy should include facilitating both the short-term and long-term scenarios such as repurposing of school buildings, constructing new ones, and availing innovative finance. In a collaborative manner, the activities to scale up global and regional long-term funding commitments could be obtained to support educational initiatives for that matter. Correspondingly, providing education during an emergency context does not mean pointing only at the formal learning domains. However, it is equally critical to take into account the need to provide non-formal education through vocational and technical training programs.

As such, education provided through non-formal means can equally contribute knowledge and practical skills for the youths to support socio-economic development. Indeed, these practical life skills are critical to be provided to the members of the society affected by conflicts. Such vocational skills include welding, bricklaying, and plumber, electrical and engineering skills, just to mention a few. These skills are very crucial in today's labor market because they can enable the school dropout youths to earn a living for themselves and support their immediate families.

Furthermore, with the provision of non-formal education, the ex-soldiers who are disarmed and demobilized could be trained and fully reintegrated into city life. Being armed with practical life skills such as building, bricklaying, plumbing and electrical skills can enable them to sustain their families, pay the tuition fees for their children and settle their medical expenses. Definitely, providing education in an emergency framework, as Cahill (2010) stresses, increases children's future earning potential, enabling them to keep their families healthier and improve their ability to leave out of the poverty cycle. This implies that the establishment of quality education during crises enables individuals to receive meaningful knowledge and practical skills for a better living both during and after crises.

Practically, it preserves the continuity of learning events and educational retention rate intact. In fact, these skills should be planned and delivered during emergency and non-emergency situations. It has become a noted fact that these days, education remains a continuous activity that goes on almost in one's continuous life. On this basis, it is imperative to evaluate key critical ideas of education and social issues that directly or indirectly affect people. No matter what kind of educational knowledge is acquired from formal or informal learning domains, it is believed that it contributes to the alleviation of poverty. On that account, reducing a high rate of illiteracy and improving the learning outcomes in the country. Not only that, but it also shapes the intellectual landscape and personal growth of an individual since acquiring knowledge is a sure gateway to a more lavish lifestyle.

In the context of South Sudan, an investment in education means a lot for the life improvement of individuals and society exclusively during the crisis. It should be mentioned that people should not wait for an emergency or any conflict to stop in order to resume the activities of the schools. In fact, the benefactors should continue to provide the necessary education and essential support in the form of knowledge and skills. This can help learners gain better knowledge and give them hope for the future to anticipate that they will one day come out of the poverty line and conflict zones.

Education as a Key Dynamic for Trust-Building and Regaining the Resiliency

In the event where wars and conflicts are fought alongside tribal and regional associations, mistrust and distrust are deeply created among the warring parties. In this sense, education practically remains an inspirational entity that can bring people together from varied works of life. As noted earlier, educational activities encourage cooperation, collaboration and nonviolent coexistence among teachers, students and educational personnel in the school community as well as in the wider society. On the other hand, students also learn interpersonal interactions and intrapersonal skills through cooperative efforts that can foster peacebuilding to gain trust and mutual confidence among themselves.

Further, the School Management Committees (SMCs) and the Parents' Teachers Associations (PTAs) are bound to work together under one umbrella to build trust and restore confidence between the school and the members of the community. In this background, education is acknowledged for its concrete reputation for disseminating knowledge and skills that can sustain one's life through regaining and maintaining resiliency. In doing so, it may minimize the distrust, loss of hope, and severer traumatic incidents the victims and the eyewitnesses might have suffered during the crises. It is the responsibility of all people to champion education for peace and protection and support quality education for better learning outcomes. Ideally, education also supports peacebuilding among the learners, school administrators and teachers both inside and outside the school environment.

Likewise, education can provide a peaceful and democratic atmosphere that will allow students of victims to focus on the appealing aspects and give them a new way to look at the world. Education is supreme, because it can overcome generational and war-based trauma which can be misleading in the learning domains if not addressed. This can possibly enable the students of the victims to forget the recent impaired memories of what had happened or is happening during the crisis. As evidenced by Cahill (2010), children and people have the opportunity to escape an environment full of tragic memories and tragic stories of what has happened to their respective families and community members. It could be admitted that children and youths who have undergone traumatic situations experience nightmares during sleep. In consequence, education can proactively keep children engaged so that they do not think of any sad reminiscences of what happened during the crisis. As far as education in an emergency context is concerned, heartbreaking memories and sad stories of the war are often cleared off when educational opportunities are provided instantly. Such provision of educational undertakings was effectively utilized well in the aftermath of the Rwandan genocide as children of Hutu and Tutsi were brought to study together under similar learning activities.

As a result, these children were to forget those miserable memories, which had happened during the genocidal war of Rwanda in 1994. In an effort to mitigate conflict within the setting of the professional community, education could also boost the delivery of quality educational services. This could be in form of more inclusive and accommodative learning environments of all learners. Put differently, education transmits a message of peace and trust-building among the learners, school personnel including the distressed groups which might have been divided along ethnic lines. Within the content delivery, teachers uniquely employ knowledge and skills to prevent violence of all forms among learners and parents at the wider community coverage.

Education as the Means for Career Guidance and Psychosocial Support

On the one hand, career guidance and psychosocial support are the fewest activities practiced in South Sudan. For obvious reasons during liberation wars, career guidance facilities and psychosocial services become non-existent. No one, either professionals or their clients, were initially interested in such unique social services; and still, it is today. For the duration of a crisis, the effects of dire situations affect people from all works of life, either directly or indirectly. On the other hand, the degree of negative impacts varies from one person and community to another. Idiosyncratically, this depends on the level of influences, destruction, and the types of political and military allegiance portrayed by the warring parties. Tragically, schools are detrimentally affected otherwise and silently either due to the death of students and teachers, on the one hand. On the other hand, parents become incredible during the crises in the event that dire circumstances become overwhelmingly uncontrollable. In such heartrending settings, education continues to be a means of providing psychosocial support services to the affected communities and individuals.

As demonstrated by Cahill (2010), education can additionally provide physical, psychosocial, and cognitive protection that can be both life-saving and life-sustaining in the description. Substantially, this is because once a school child loses one of their parents, they would start developing hatred and segregation towards their other colleagues whose tribes might be considered as offenders due to war related crimes. Ardently, the children of the victims are likely to detach and withdraw their interpersonal relationships from their colleagues whose parents or tribemates might have committed grave abuses of human rights. For this reason, such situations may create a hostile but also conducive learning intellectually.

In a multi-ethnic state like South Sudan, which is divided along ethnic and political lines, education remains a critical factor to be applied for reconciliation and the peaceful coexistence of learners. Exclusively, education should build a pluralistic society that aims to adopt one traditional, political and economic agenda. As pointed out by Cole (2007), the national task is to accommodate former enemies, rather than political opponents, and to reestablish vibrant and functioning social institutions and political and inclusive systems of all communities. This is precisely, in line with democratic education to provide informed and educated citizens irrespective of their political and ethnic associations.

Holistically, education almost remains the notable societal value to be acquired so as to contribute to peace and an all-inclusive society regardless of ethnic, cultural, and political differences. In the presence of wars and ethnic divisions in a country, healing and reconciliation become unachievable. However, education, if it is widely applied and expanded rationally at all community levels, can restore justice that streamlines the fair distribution of resources. This exclusively can build trust and confidence among diverse ethnic communities. Because of the fact that ethnic division, distrust, and exclusivity of minority groups in the political and economic dispensation have taken deep and wider roots, the healing and counseling process takes the lead in such situations. This can be done by providing guidance and counseling services to the affected population on how to coexist together.

Invariably, strategizing on counselling services is important in a dire situation that is unflattering in terms of conflict expansion and polarization of tribes along ethnic lines. This is in line with the argument put forward by Cole (2007) that the process of healing and transformation is typically complicated by the legacy of trauma and the fragility of social infrastructures and political institutions. This means that traumatic incidents can happen during the war and will continue to disturb the minds of the affected individuals. Without interventions being carried out earlier, it can be challenging to avoid the hypothetical and complicated negative consequences in one's life in the more overdue times and spaces.

On the other hand, education still plays a vital role in disseminating important life messages and skills during and after the crises. In fact, most of the learners and their teachers get confused about what to perform during crises. However, the provision of some pieces of training can support them to disseminate relatable messages in relation to protecting individuals from being victims of the wars. Optimally, teachers should be able to decide on the right way to uphold teaching profession, such as keeping away from military training and forceful recruitment into the fighting forces. Uniformly, teachers ought to be trained as transitory counsellors to enable them use their knowledge and skills as a critical basis for conflict transformation and peace education in the school settings.

Definitely, this will enable the reinforcement of coping skills, expression of learning interests, and economic ideals between the learners and the school personnel. From an emergency perspective, a number of educational activities are carried out in line with the educational policy to help those children trapped in conflict-stricken societies. In this setting, education becomes a worthwhile tool to keep the children and youth informed of their health and hygienic conditions. This is observably mentioned by Cahill (2010) who pointed out that education can additionally provide learners with knowledge and skills to survive in a crisis through the dissemination of life-saving information about deadly landmines. In line of this, efforts for education can help disseminate safety precautions about cluster bombs, HIV/AIDS prevention, conflict-resolution mechanisms and peacebuilding among the others. Indeed, many learners have become victims of landmines and explosives across South Sudan due to unabated carelessness and parental ignorance.

During conflict, health and hygienic conditions become crucial factors causing death or causing life complications to children and youth affected by conflict and other war-related diseases. In a range of different social contexts, it is imperative to train the youths on the basic skills relevant to health and hygienic issues. In this essence, it means that during crises, a lot of hygienic and health issues resurface. On that account, this may add some complications and suffering to the people who are already engulfed in political turmoil or natural disasters. By the same token, education creates a favorable learning environment for socio-economic means and efforts that empower youths and families at local and national levels.

As economic hardships intensify, education becomes the least to be desired by the youths and adults to get skills and knowledge for survival. More importantly, providing a conducive and protective learning environment with educational and economic opportunities could encourage learners to move away from traumatic events. This is because if the commonness of emotional injuries endured during the war as a result of adverse effects is not healed immediately, they would remain unhealed among learners and parents in their respective communities.

In light of this mere claim, it is socially binding that psychological aspects can be emotionally challenging to people particularly the youths and adults whose economic power is least desirable and manageable. In most cases, this inference demonstrates the degree of dynamic emotional tensions that need prompt attention to advance effective intervention strategies through education as a means for conflict extenuation. Admittedly, the aim of psychosocial support activities is to encourage the affected people by conflict to restore hope and social dignity within and outside their neighborhood. It is moreover, a means to improve the psychological and social well-being of the affected population. This enables them to achieve a calmed life with a well-integrated functioning system. Indeed, psychological support programs are strategies aimed at addressing both the psychological and social needs of the affected communities. To this point, schools deserve social activities to be strategized and prioritized in emergency-stricken locations. If psychological support programs are organized and immediately rendered, the emotional situations among the learners and their children could be normalized.

Education as a Form of Investment for Human Resource Development

School community during crises provides protection for learners and their teachers. In order to provide quality life during the emergency and non-emergency situations, it is integrally critical and rationally sensible to develop and implement the elements of professional capital for teachers and school personnel. Workwise, such professional development should be geared towards developing human, social and decisional capacities to handle the hostile learning environment for effective educational outcomes. More recent studies have pointed out that professional capital is an essential component in classroom settings in relation to enhancing the capacity of the teaching force. For instance, Fullan (2016) asserts that professional capital contains three distinct but corresponding elements namely human capital, social capital, and decisional capital.

Practically, he stresses that human capital focuses on the quality of an individual. This means that quality workforce should be encouraged in order to realize quality learning and a desired professional outcome. In addition, social capital centers on the quality of the group and the employees. These all depend upon capacity building programmes to be initiated in order to support institutional functionality. As a final point, decisional capital stresses the quality based on decisions and expert judgment. Quality decisions enable teachers, and other school personnel to perform exceptionally while delivering learning activities during crises. Developing such distinctive capitals during the crisis is an indication of improving the professional community.

In the light of decisional capital, it is imperative that interactive learning and teaching domain is very much highlighted. This may lead to the quality of what the teaching force aims to achieve within the school leadership. It is vital that such key development areas within the school settings are fundamentally reinforcing the school leadership. However, key development areas in terms of knowledge and skills are apparently overlooked in many conflict situations. In this perspective, EiE is a clash in practice since the acquisition of knowledge and skill is least desired in South Sudan. Notwithstanding, knowledge and expertise on the subject matter by the teachers are crucially important in the face of crisis. So, fostering teacher learning to improve the quality of instruction is advantageously desired but vocally emphasized. As yet, these factors of professional development have been hailed to have improved and lifted the phases of challenges facing humankind in different economic, political, social, and geographical spheres, at the global level.

In this way, neglecting these vibrant components of life to develop a professional community would largely affect the performance of the government in the course of implementing its national plans and school agenda. Henceforth, the quality outcomes of educational activities could continue to be a daunting challenge in the face of crises, if vital steps are not applied to address them. For this reason, advancing professional capital should be deliberately in threefold: managerial skills, training and recruiting qualified teachers across the country, as well as providing quality education. In terms of managerial skills, it is apparent that many school personnel might lack administrative skills and technical expertise to run the school effectively even when engulfed in a hostile situation. This is because handling such complicated situations lacks expert knowledge in education in emergencies rather than harsh policies imposed by force by the government.

Substantially, education is a lively tool designed to combat the basic problems of human beings such as poverty, conflicts, and unemployment. This is because education imbues individuals with inquisitiveness and intellectual understanding. Generally, this points to necessity of providing good learning atmosphere for the professional growth of learners. It is worth noticing that both learners and teachers ought to practice and appreciate sincerity and sympathy within and outside the school settings. This alone encourages peaceful settlements to flourish among the members of disparate ethnic groups in a given neighborhood; therefore, this implies that achieving educational goals is manageable. On the other hand, recruiting qualified manpower is reliable affirmative action. However, these should remain the types of people who have undergone vigorous teacher training and have gained massive administrative and teaching experiences. In fact, the recruitment of quality schoolteachers will result in the creation of a conducive learning environment that persuades and encourages learners.

To a larger extent, trained teachers can push for the continuity of the schooling by devising better mechanisms and technical know-how that can enable the school to operate uninterruptedly. It is imperative that well organized training activities and capacity building programs can help teachers respond to other burdens during crises. Unequivocally, imparted skills support teachers to cope with increased responsibilities and ultimately see themselves and their surroundings as resources required to achieve the school mission. The teacher training is required to equip and refresh them with the technical knowledge and skills to implement the needs-based teaching activities and adequately support teachers.

More importantly, Smith (2009) believes that education remains the means of transmitting cultural and societal values from one generation to the other with regards to discouraging negative stereotypes which may cause conflict as well as dispensing positive attitudes that cannot condone conflict. In a situation where conflict follows an ethnic turn, education carries out a pivotal role in discouraging a negative atmosphere for both the teachers and the learners. As conflict intensifies, many learners would be able to regroup themselves on the basis of tribes, regional or political associations. This is already a dangerous social path, in which education should be geared towards discouraging such negative endeavors and inappropriate behaviors.

To put it simply, some would argue that education trains the youth particularly and the public in general in order to foster and promote national and cultural identities. From the transitional period (2005-2011) and the subsequent independence of the Republic of South Sudan from the rest of Sudan on July 9th, 2011, to date, one would be convinced that the education system in South Sudan has not achieved its intended educational goals. Why is this? The answer points to the universal education program created by the government which sometimes ends up in corruption and diversion of educational funds. In a shambling event, although the provision of educational opportunities during the emergency and non-emergency situations has become a major concern in rural and urban setups. This is the focus of the book to highlight some or all the educational issues related to emergency crises. Indeed, the book places more emphasis on the challenges, which clearly affect the school environment and the community around them. In addition, the book aims to explore practical mechanisms on how to devise means and experiences to address the challenges besetting the national educational system, here and now.

Smith (2009) has clearly demonstrated that education can also offer critical messages and skills that enable learners to overcome their daily problems. In addition, education avoids many shreds of challenges such as avoiding recruitment into the armed forces, learners being abducted or being exposed to sexual and gender exploitations. To be sure, teaching and disseminating life-saving messages and life-sustaining ideas to school children and teachers are the major need for education in an emergency context. With this approach intact, the learners will be thoroughly informed with the daily updates on how to stay safe and healthy in the time of crises.

Back to necessities, discipline in the classroom environment produces rigorous academics and professionals who think and behave maturely like global citizens. This is because schooling is predominantly designed in a manner to meet the intellectual and accomplished goals of the learners in given geographical locations and cultural frameworks. Honestly speaking, I strongly believe that schooling can provide safe learning and teaching spaces, psychosocial and emotional development of the learners during crises. Sensibly, an encouraging learning environment can be supplemented by offering opportunities for learners to receive school-feeding programs and medical services since these are some of the components of the primary needs.

On the contrary, the schools should be encouraged and supported financially to provide feeding programs for all the schools. School feeding program is an initiative to provide lunch for children during the day to minimize hunger among the learners. This can enable learners to concentrate on their teaching and learning activities while at the school propositions. This can on top applies to the provision of medical and first aid supplies for the teaching and non-teaching staff as well as the students. It is also an integral part that school constitutes the second-best home for the learner to provide a range of diversified learning environments, emotional and moral development of the learners. Provision of essential services is itself the protection of learners from insecurities as some may go to some distance in search of medical services. In so doing, they may end up either being killed, raped, or abducted by the armed forces.

As far as the learning environment is concerned, EiE requires to be operated in a democratic and supportive atmosphere so that teaching and learning activities are not compromised. As I have emphasized earlier, establishing private learning institutions adds a great weight not only to the education system but also to the titleholders who own the schools. To recognize this reality, such social and economic platforms for financial investment on the side of the community members who send their children to school to be educated become a decisive course of action.

Education is a Shield for Protecting Educational Facilities and Tangible Resources

Schools must always remain peaceful and active zones for children to learn. Making learning institutions operational typically implies the adequate protection of learning facilities and educational assets. As reported by Mundy and Sarah (2011), the moral standards were typically developed in a participatory way, drawing on existing good practices and field-based experiences with realistic targets. This illustrates that the designed minimum standard provides all somewhat protection in all learning environments. In so doing, it ensures that learning spaces are secure to promote the mental and moral well-being of learners, teachers, and other educational personnel.

Significantly, South Sudan Minimum Standards also recommend the key provision of equitable educational opportunities for innocent boys and typical girls in humanitarian emergencies.

This is considered essential to ensure that not only girls maintain equal access to the economic benefits of education, but also the entire school-going age children equally deserve better educational prospects. It is also reported that the minimum standard encouraged the inclusion of relevant learning content, which is related to peacebuilding, conflict resolution and mitigation. Not to mention the vulnerability of girls who are exposed to sexual violence and labor exploitation is more widely acknowledged as a violation of human rights and a crime against humanity. In addition, gender equality and gender protection concerns are much emphasized to continue a static target in all aspects of education in emergencies and chronic crises. This on tops applies to the prevailing contexts prior reconstruction of the destroyed concrete materials and emotional wellbeing of the society.

Properly aligned to addressing complex challenges and go-ahead circumstances facing the education sector, the commitments made in human rights and other legal instruments and targets, like the Convention on the Rights of the Child (CRC), the Education for All (EFA), and Millennium Development Goals (MDGs) should be implemented in the letter and spirit. So far, minimum standards have ensured equal access to education, learning content, processes, and the interactions between teachers and students. A controversial issue is the moderate component of education that needs a great deal of attention as far as attaining gender equality is concerned.

Rationally speaking, preparedness, recovery, and response remain the global tools that articulate the minimum level with regards to the quality of education and similar access to determining opportunities. In this essence, it should be mentioned that these comprehensive tools are aimed to upsurge a safe and supportive learning environment, encourage continuity and completion rates of the learners at any level of education. Despite possible conflicts, academic preparedness and rapid response strategies are steadfastly maintained to enthusiastically support the learning opportunities in urban and rural settings. In an emergency scene, continued access to education can reduce the psychosocial impact of conflict on children by giving them a sense of normalcy and hope for the future.

PART THREE

Negative Impressions Toward Education in the Time of Crises

Recruitment of Learners and Educational Personnel into the Armed Forces

In times of emergencies, there are potential and discernable impacts of disaster-related phenomena that face learners and school workforces. As a result of war, the recruitment of students and teachers into the armed forces become the usual and work-related concerns. It is a disturbing fact that recruiting teachers and students render the schools to be non-operational and tangibly isolated. Both teachers and students become vulnerable to conscription either into the national armed forces or insurgent allied forces. In fact, armed groups target children for several reasons. Being poor, displaced, separated from their families to live in a combat zone can make children particularly vulnerable to target recruitments.

It is noticeably observed that children and minorities may be required to participate in harrowing training or initiation ceremonies, to undergo hazardous labor. Alternatively, they are engage in active combat with great risk of death, chronic injury and disability. They may also witness, suffer or be forced to take part in torture and killings in all sorts of military fitness activities. Regardless of how children are recruited and of their roles, child soldiers are victims, whose participation in conflict bears serious implications for their physical and emotional well-being. Ensuring respect for the rights of children is a top priority. Hence, school activities from security-wise are almost threatened and continuously rendered least functional to attract learners. One illustration of this view is that Machel (2001) has estimated that about 300,000 children less than 18 years old were involved as fighters, cooks, porters, informants, sex slaves, laboring roles with government armies, paramilitaries, and rebel groups in some countries like Colombia, Israel, Myanmar, Sri Lanka, and Uganda (as cited in Lisa, 2012). In fact, armed recruitment either forcefully or willingly is a common practice in conflict-prone nations.

In the context of South Sudan, the Office of the Coordination of the Humanitarian Affairs (OCHA, 2018), about 128 child soldiers as disaggregated of 90 are boys and 38 are girls were associated with the two armed forces of the South Sudan National Liberation Movement (SSNLM) and the Sudan People's Liberation Army in Opposition (SPLA-IO) after the 2016 crisis. Conversely, they were officially released in August 2018 at Yambio in former Western Equatoria State and rejoined with their immediate parents and guardians. Moreover, it has been observed that an estimated 9,000 children were recruited into the armed forces as fighting child soldiers following the outbreak of the 2013 civil war in South Sudan (Mayai, & Hammond, 2014). For instance, in South Sudan, many cases of child soldiers have been reported for both parties to the conflict in the previous and current civil wars. In light of recruiting child soldiers into the fighting forces, it remains clear that schools are emptied since the school-going age boys and girls are recruited into the combat units.

On this provision to release child soldiers, it is a wise idea in order to help them to be rejoined with their parents or guardians, whilst also gaining the opportunity to enroll in school once again. Persuasively, this confirmatory action is a motion of good will for the armed forces since it may pave the way for the activities of education in emergencies to prevail in violent conflict or disaster-affected regions. In fact, recruitment of child soldiers into regular and irregular forces is a war crime and crime against humanity. In light of this claim, South Sudan has been accused on multiple fronts of cases related to a child soldier. Of course, some may object that there are indicators of child recruitment in South Sudan, but the reality is that massive child recruitment has been witnessed from different opposing armed groups across the country.

From my standpoint, such activities of recruiting the school community into the armed forces are out-of-the-way habits, which need to be legally debarred. It should be followed with strong condemnation nationwide by the domestic governments and with help of the international community. Therefore, schools should be suitable grounds for keeping children safe and academically engaged as an alternative means of retaining and keeping learners in the school. This can contribute to learners' continuity of learning, hence leading to the successful completion of a given educational cycle. Certainly, this is bad practice by the government and rebel groups to recruit child soldiers into their militaries instead of going to school.

As noted by Human Rights Watch (HRW, 2005), children who were demobilized in Liberia, were recruited into the Militia of Cote d'Ivoire and were later attracted back into the militia by the promise of economic incentives to buy food, pay rent, school fees, or health care cost (as cited in Lisa, 2012). This implies that children are mostly attracted to the armed forces by simple things such as food, besides the need to hunt for their tuition fees. At some points, soldiers also offer other favorable outlooks and economic prospects for children affected by conflict to be attracted to the barracks and military units.

Despite challenges facing the education sector in times of crisis, it is imperative that rapid response strategies could be employed as practicable tools aimed at prioritizing emergency activities and preparedness planning as the first step. Such activities of EiE should include the provision of a conducive learning environment that protects the teachers, students, and school infrastructures. Technically, a protective and safe learning environment is a comfort zone not only for learners but also for the wider community. Moreover, EIE can help in the rehabilitation of schools damaged, and those destroyed during emergencies. The move can also be extended to include judicious advocacy initiatives against the occupation of schools by armed groups. In a similar vein, establishment of temporary learning spaces (TLS) in schools which are a bit overcrowded to give space for those learners who are learning outdoor. In the same approach, provision of psychosocial support activities in the context of crisis such as guidance and counseling behaviors, career and emotional development of the learners, the teaching of life-saving masses, and life-sustaining information is one of the best alternatives to save education during crises.

As far as considering education as a basic human right is concerned, the South Sudanese youths and children have been manipulated by their country's political leadership with or without their knowledge. Practically, this ultimately points to the reality that wars that have been ongoing in the country are being fought by a large portion of the country's youth population below the age of 40 years. In this regard, it implies that they are either recruited forcefully or willingly, thus, their future is potentially undermined. This begs a necessity that the more recruitment of youths and adults into the armed forces, the more their future is potentially ruined and economically rendered impractical. Along similar lines, the study conducted and analyzed by Mayai and Hammond (2014), revealed that the generations of the South Sudanese being affected by war may probably be mobilized into the armed forces and violent factions. This may deprive them of their right to acquire fundamental socio-economic knowledge and skills that are crucially vital for building a sustainable future.

In sharp contrast, the UN Office for the Coordination of Humanitarian Affairs (OCHA) has estimated that nearly 2 million people have become victims of the conflicts and nearly 13, 000 children were recruited into the armed forces and armed groups in South Sudan (Vaessen, Diaz, Ekaterina, & Arushi, 2016). This suggests that socio-economic sustainability among the youths is pushed aside and thus, no meaningful future is expected of them due to lack of the acquired maintainable knowledge and skills for building substantial communities. In reality, most of the learners who have no other options are left to join the fighting in order to protect themselves as well as getting food for a living. In light of this fact, the implication tells us that these youths may lose their rights to education, and this may potentially affect them when it comes to accessing job opportunities.

In certain terms, it may be said that a few of the youths who oppose the idea of armed recruitment and instead prefer education have high chances to secure a sustainable way of life to succeed in life expectancy. However, the idea to join the school as the best method to acquire knowledge and skills during crises could remain intact, sustainable, and professional reassuring. From the literacy and numeracy point of view, Mali and Pakistan both have higher literacy rates than South Sudan. As a result of continuous war, the biggest portion of the population remains illiterate and economically vulnerable. Indeed, schools and other learning institutions were negatively affected by series of conflict that has engulfed the country since then. In fact, an emergency remains an issue of concern to the world leaders and the general public when it strikes unexpectedly. Henceforth, educational centers are largely affected per se.

On the other hand, inadequate implementation of the government's policy to allow unhindered access of girls and young women to equal educational opportunities remains a worrying situation. In the analysis of different government policies to implement girls' education, Cahill (2010) has observed that the barriers to girl child education around the world may be equally present in most fragile states. This is due to the fact that the reluctance and inability of the state to implement gender and targeted girl education strategies remains an alarming constituent. The policy on girl education in South Sudan states that every member of the community has equal participation in the educational processes at all levels. In support of this principle, Sommers (2004) has contended that a considerate government could extend educational services to its refugees stranded in expatriate schools of the host countries through the provision of textbooks and other educational resources. Surprisingly, such concerns are non-applicable in fragile states where the government is not able to finance the educational activities and programs for girls caught up by conflict in fragile states.

Emergencies Contribute to Educational Wastages

Educational wastage is a wide-reaching phenomenon which has negatively affected the education system of the developing countries. Educational wastage implies the inefficient use of educational resources to produce graduates with quality educational knowledge and skills. Some of the noticeable signs of educational wastage include dropouts, repeaters, premature withdrawals, misguided types of education, non- employment of school leavers and even brain drain. It occurs due to dropping out of students from the educational institutions, before completion of the prescribed learning cycle. In addition, educational wastage implies the reality in which the educational programs of study and their educational skills are not honed. It also applies to the repetition of classes, and educational courses are being unsuccessful in academic performances, hence leading to educational stagnation.

Educational wastage exists in various forms such as the failure of the institutional systems to provide a universal education for all. Equally substantial, educational wastage implies a lack of recruitment of children into the system and hold them within the system. Educational wastage also implies the failure of the system to set appropriate learning objectives and inefficiency in the achievement of national educational goals. Educational wastage implies producing graduates with less knowledge and skills relevant to the job market. As far as education is concerned, socio-economic poverty, inequality of sexes, illiteracy, rampant superstitions, conservative attitudes are some of the main causes for school dropouts. Likewise, paucity of funds and their improper distribution also aggravate the problem as higher classes may not be added to the schooling environment.

On a similar account, overcast and unpleasant schools, inefficient and poor quality of teachers, defective examinations, and unexciting curricula, lack of proper parental attitude and care, and absence of school health services are primarily responsible for educational wastage. On a similar vein, when individuals have obtained good quality education and are unable to make use of their skills and abilities to promote the well-being of the community and sustain their living conditions is also treated as a direct educational wastage.

Equally important, education certainly determines the quality of an individual's life. Education improves one's knowledge, skills and develops the personality and attitude. Most noteworthy, Education affects the chances of employment for people. A highly educated individual is probably very likely to get a good job. Having education in an area helps people think, feel, and behave in a way that contributes to their success and improves not only their personal satisfaction but also their community. In addition, education develops human personality, thoughts, dealing with others and prepares people for life experiences. For children in emergencies, education is about more than the right to learn. Schools protect children from the physical dangers around them which may include child abuse, exploitation and recruitment into armed groups. They provide children with lifesaving food, water, health care and hygiene supplies. It can save lives by creating safe learning environments within the spaces established for formal and non-formal educational activities. Education can also protect learners against exploitation and harm, and lessen the chances that children will be recruited into fighting groups or gangs or become victims of sexual violence.

At the first glance, in many war-affected countries around the globe where laws of protecting girl child marriage remain ineffective, many girls often become vulnerable to child marriages. On similar note, others become victims of community gender-based related aspects, especially among the pastoralist communities where girls are wealthily priced. On the other hand, the situation of underage marriage among girls of school-going age becomes increasingly prevalent when crises hit the nation where they are married off against their will. In South Sudan in particular, this apparent business has been encouraged and supported by either parents or guardians, just because of their economic standing and social interests.

According to Mundy and Sarah (2011), early marriage is a strategy in which the parents adopt to protect their daughters, but one that usually results in premature school dropout. For obvious reasons, girls are married off as early as 14 years of age in South Sudan in particular and other developing countries in general. This is not just a made-up statement but a reality on the ground especially among the pastoral communities where underage girl marriage is highly valued and priced. Under certain family practices and social arrangements, a female child becomes a victim of early marriage when the right suitor turns up with a good herd of cattle, goats, sheep, cash, or other valuable materials. In such a situation, the girl is left with no option, but to accept what the parents have to say about her future without a question or resistant explanation. In other words, though such girls detest forced and child marriage, they would give in just in cultural compliance with respect to their parents. It has become an evident-based fact that in some parts of South Sudan, the birth of a girl is widely celebrated more than the birth of a boy. Still, up to date, some communities consider girls as the potential source of family wealth in terms of bride price and other linked economic proceeds.

During conflict situations, it is noticeable in some parts of the communities that parents could no longer allow their daughters to continue with their education as they consider them as family assets to be priced. From the community perspective, girls are maximally protected more than boys. As such, they are groomed and shaped to be resourceful family possessions and that they would be kept indoors during any crisis in an effort to secure the potential wealth in terms of bride price. Ultimately, this creates a gap in girl education as far as literacy and numeracy boosts are concerned in South Sudan. Conversely, teenage pregnancy is one of the main challenges during conflict and non-conflict situations. The protection for girls during conflict becomes limited as they are likely to end up pregnant due to sexual violence. This insinuates that once a girl becomes pregnant at young age, chances are high for the girl to drop out of school in order to take care of her child. Indeed, this creates a wider gap in girl education in many parts of the country. In learning reality, there is a high rate of gender disparity in all educational levels in South Sudan due to the early pregnancy of girls that leads to subsequent high rate of school dropout.

According to United Nations, Educational, Scientific, and Cultural Organizations Statistics (UNESCO, 2004), conflict and emergencies have particular implications for girls and seriously compromise the possibilities for educational systems to meet the needs of girls and women (as cited in Mundy & Sarah, 2011).

Based on such implications, it is obvious that gender equality in the education sector is undermined completely by so many obvious reasons some of which have been lengthily discussed in this book. This implies that conflict and other emergency contexts negatively impact girl education given the vulnerability of girls and women in most societies. In other words, most of the girls and women become victims of rape, abduction, forced marriage, as well as being brutally exposed to gender-based violence. These are apparent cases around the globe that have been used as weapons of war by the warring parties. For instance, in most conflict-affected regions such as Equatoria and Upper Nile, in which three-quarters of girls remain out of the schools. This denotes that most boys and girls become victims since the schools are occupied by soldiers as well as displacement of communities could become the order of the day.

On the contrary, the fact that a big number of adults being present on the streets of major towns in South Sudan including Juba may possibly contribute to educational wastage per se. I use the term educational wastage in this book to define those who drop out of school as a result of forced marriage, unwanted pregnancies, recruitment to armed forces, class repetition, and other reasons as a result of continuous wars and tribal conflicts. Educational wastage will continue to be felt in South Sudan unless collective efforts are put together to curb the school dropout rates.

The Inescapabilty of Poverty and Economic Hardships for Learners and Parents

Though there is already a big gap created by poverty and economic hardships in the country, more wars or other related calamities prevent people from being more productive. For instance, about 4.6 million people are affected by severe food shortages during the South Sudanese Conflict (Vaessen et al., 2016). In fact, this is true to some extent because when conflicts strike, most of the communities no longer produce enough food due to various war factors hindering their access. On the same note, economic hardships hinder education for girls and boys because parents cannot afford the education of their daughters during the crisis.

Child soldiers are easily manipulated, they do not need much food and they may develop a sense of danger in major military barracks. There could be a shortage of food, a lack of clothing, much disease, and homelessness. In addition, they are commonly subject to labor abuse and most of them witness death, killing, and sexual violence. Child soldiers are more often killed or injured than adult soldiers on the front line. They are less costly for the respective group or organization than adult recruits, because they receive fewer resources, including less and smaller weapons and equipment. It is vital that providing a secure environment where children have ways of being safe, well fed and properly clothed that do not involve carrying a gun is something to which all of us can and must contribute. Much as girl education is concerned, poverty has remained one of the biggest issues that thwart girl education countrywide. Because of frequent protracted civil wars, poverty becomes imminent among ordinary citizens due to displacement and lack of concentration of major economic efforts and agricultural activities for the survival of the respective communities.

In the investigation carried out by Mundy and Sarah, (2011), fragile states are rarely in a position to provide gender-responsive education due to discriminative curricula and minimal resources. As a result of a lack of support and supervision for teachers and head teachers, this squarely leads to gender inequalities. In South Sudan, gender inequalities both in public and private domains have been an issue of concern. For obvious reasons, women's place has been viewed as the kitchen in some communities and so education becomes the last priority for women. Outwardly, it could be admitted that if a family is poor, food and other basic necessities take preference before scholastic materials can be purchased. In light of the current conflict in South Sudan, there exists a gender component as both boys and girls are affected together. However, the girls are affected more than boys due to their weaker position in their respective communities. For instance, with little resources available in the family, the parents always prefer the education of boys to girls. This decision by parents to discriminate the education of girls as equal members of the respective families and the community alike.

From the economic outlook, the productive force is affected, and this leads to low-quality workforces being demanded by the local markets. Viewing it from agronomic undertakings, it could be admitted that, other income-generating activities are affected by the conflict. As a result, poverty has hit the whole country, and learning institutions are affected negatively in terms of school fees, as the parents are no longer able to afford the education of their children besides other family needs. As such, Mundy and Sarah (2011) have pointed out those children affected by conflict at school age rarely attend school and complete a full basic education cycle, and are much less likely to gain access to secondary education. This is a clear indication in South Sudan where a high rate of school dropout is widespread across the country.

In the South Sudan context, economic hardship has usually been a measure of transitory income deprivation, which are highly dominated by a material hardship. Economic hardships can also be caused by a lack of employment opportunities, unstable employment or precarious work as a result of breakdown of economic viability. Financial hardship is uncontrollable for all civil servants since they do not meet the cost of basic food commodity because of a high purchasing power in the local markets. Because of protracted conflicts, substantial fluctuations in the value of local currency exchange rate has negatively affected the performance of national education system. Indeed, unexpected changes in the financial condition of the learners and their parents have limited the source of support, medical bills, or other substantial and unexpected expenses.

Throughout the world history, women have been marginalized and oppressed (still are today) by men because of their weaker position as disadvantaged minority in the society. In most cases, many people consider women as sex objects who are only kept to carry out home responsibilities rather than national duties. From the perspectives of some communities, women have no rights to own property or speak out their minds for the social and political things that matter a lot in a society. The underestimation of the importance, competency, and capability of women has been taken for granted and nobody seems to care more about them. The fact is, some men do not care much about the welfare of their women (including girls) simply because they are ignorant of them as people with no contribution in the community and treat them as minor personalities with minor roles to play in the social and political arenas.

According to the Universal Declaration of Human Rights (article 2), everyone is entitled to all the rights and freedoms set forth in this Declaration, without distinction of any kind, such as race, color, sex, language, religion, political or other opinion, national or social origin, property, birth or other status. The Human Rights declaration is universally applicable to every member of human society living as part and parcel of humankind in the male-dominated world. The law implies that all women including girls should be treated equally alongside with their male counterparts since they have the same sense and feelings of belonging to the human race.

In this context, men should be mindful and respectful of women in their capacities as dutiful mothers and wives in this planet. In fact, women have thousand roles to play both at homes, in schools, hospitals, business centers, government and private institutions. In reality, women are full-time custodians of home affairs, effective managers, child-caregivers, security personnel of their husbands and children, nation peacemakers, non-warmongers, democracy and human rights promoters, as well as being resourceful citizens taken away in exchange of wealth in form of bride price. In this spirit, women must enjoy the same equal status in society both in the political, social, and economic spheres of life. It would be no-nonsense if the country's leadership should do something tangible on the grounds for women to be fully absorbed in the public and private fields so as to upgrade their leadership positions.

Furthermore, women are sometimes culturally-oriented aware to observe the importance of the cultural identities within and outside the society. In many aspects, cultures are the ways of life of people, and all members of the society are obligatorily obliged to observe them on daily basis. However, men sometimes become reluctant and women in this context remind their children about the roles and to make sure that children strictly follow the norms and traditions set up by a given society. Equally, women groom and orient their daughters into responsible members of the society. Even a woman who is a minister in the government or state cabinet can still come back home after work and present herself as mother and wife in the house.

Conversely, women are real peace makers in the wider community because of their humility, patience, and meekness. For instance, a woman carries a child for nine months before bringing it into the world. The bottom-line reality is that, women are always concerned and compassionate about the suffering and hardships experienced by human beings. Having witnessed the level of destruction the country has gone through, still is, they often feel concern about the destruction of both human and material resources. In this essence, they are much bothered about the wellbeing of their sons and daughters who are dying as a result of war and other associated consequences.

To remind you the important roles women can play in both political, economic, and social lives, here find the typical examples of some women who turned out to be national and international figures in the academic and political circles. Briefly, let look at some of the achievements of Dr. Julia Aker, the former undersecretary of the Ministry of Parliamentarian Affairs, former Vice Chancellor of Dr. John Garang Memorial University, and now the Undersecretary of the Ministry of Public Services and Human Resource Development. In her capacity as an educated woman, Dr. Julia Aker came up with a project aims at sponsoring women for masters' Degree at Indiana University for the first batch and currently the second batch had pursued its studies at the University of Juba. Being an educated woman gave her a better chance to put into use her ideas and convince donors and the well-wishers to fund her project for the benefit and the good of her common south Sudanese. The United States Agencies for International Development (USAID) in this case could not waste its time but took the initiative seriously and funded it with millions of dollars in an attempt to promote women position and leadership in the developing countries including South Sudan.

However, no man has neither done that nor willing to do it. The graduates of the first batch of her project are now lecturers in public Universities in South Sudan serving thousands of students, while others are serving the government in various departments. Meanwhile, the second batch has successfully completed its studies at the University of Juba under the same program and now being absorbed to serve their communities at different capacities as teachers, managers, lecturers or education officers. This is just an idea from one woman and if all south Sudanese women are educated, I am sure South Sudan would have been at different levels of human resource and economic development. This is what I can call an enormous achievement designed by one woman and is now realized as an important idea which is beneficial for all South Sudanese as far as eradication of illiteracy and promotion of women leadership are concerned.

Moreover, there are other educated women elites who are performing well both in the private and public sectors. The typical women who are presenting themselves as role models to young girls in the public domains include the current Speaker of the South Sudan's Transitional Legislative Assembly, Cde Jemma Nunu Kumba and Hon. Awut Deng Achuil, Minister of General Education and Instruction. Both personalities are some important national figures who are unequivocally rendering quality services to their people. The above-mentioned women leaders are among hundreds of women who are fully committed to serve their country and their people in good faith. Nobody would challenge their capabilities and personalities in their various assignments and that they do not discriminate against people of other nationalities because they consider all people from all works of life as their own biological children.

In the African continent setting, the roles of women are always underestimated in all the spheres of life and is completely a different case in South Sudan where women particularly rural women have no choice of human and individual rights. This is because of the assumption that women are weak in minds to make critical decisions in their lives. This is not true, and a person who has that assumption seems to be an isolated one from this modern world of new discoveries of new ideas. To understand how women, think and compete in socio-economic spheres of life, first look how girls compete in the academic lines with their male counterparts. Some girls even become brighter more than boys in a context that sometimes boys consult them how to write English compositions or sorting out arithmetic calculations including other academic assignments. In the family, a girl and her brother go to the same school and spend the hours learning the same content. Nevertheless, when they come back home, all of them feel exhausted but still a girl can make it to the kitchen to prepare meal for the family and brings it to the table for her siblings and other family members to enjoy. This industriousness of a girl indicates that women are as competent and capable as men in the wider community. Nothing that men can do and women cannot do in this universe.

Otherwise all human beings have the same and equal characteristics and competencies all over the world. What is needed most is the education and training of both men and women by imparting to them both life-saving and life-enhancing information so that they can contribute to the economic and political development of their country. By considering the dutiful roles, the south Sudanese women carry out, one would conclude that women are as capable and competent as men and the government and well-wishers should protect their rights and consider equal representation with equal pay both in the political and economic spheres of life.

By comparative advantage, education of girls is very important for the country because the future will be brighter and better in terms of social prospects and professional improvement. In an equal footing, national economy may grow faster if more women are educated, they become financially strong, thus, reducing level of poverty and solve widespread health related issues. In addition, educated women take proper care of their children and the families in terms parental care, providing good hygienic conditions, as well as realizing professional predispositions and social progress.

Displacement of Students and the School Community

During emergency, observe consequences are typically widespread, and this includes displacement of people and their property. Displacement can lead to interrupted schooling, hence a large number of children who struggle to access and persist in school may miss their learning opportunities. Further, local areas in which refugees and internally displace persons typically live are frequently the most neglected constituencies with an apparent lack of complimentary access to essential services including schooling infrastructure. Typically, a displaced learner in common is any student who lacks an established, regular, and adequate nighttime residence and is also coupled with a lack of continuity of learning. Despite the displacement of the learners and teachers, school community relationship is still intact, and a mutual understanding is required. During humanitarian crises, the school and the community link with each other for the outstanding achievement of ultimate goals of the community and school too. Established school realistically is a social organization which functions properly on the effective interrelationship within itself and with its associate communities.

On positive account, public-spirited crises can efficiently be formidable barriers to achieving the Sustainable Development Goals of inclusive and equitable education for all. When learners and their fond parents are forcibly displaced from their historic homes and local communities due to civil war or inevitable disaster, they typically face numerous challenges in naturally acquiring quality education. Many learners miss out in years of schooling in their displacement and subsequent struggle to be safe and secure. When children grow up in a terrible mode of gradual displacement, their education is often interrupted either entirely or partially inevitable. Internally displaced children have not shared in the considerable all-inclusive improvements in complimentary access to education in the past two established decades, and they all too often remain without adequate schooling.

It is apparent in many fragile states that when an emergency strikes, standard displacement of learners, school personnel, and the broader community is proportionately witnessed across the developing country. Like the ultimate destruction of school facilities, displacement of parents with their children during conflict is one of the contributing negative impressions that are typically triggered by possible conflicts. In any conflict situation, vulnerable groups such as women and girls are ousted to where there are no schools. However, this is very disturbing and clearly violates girls' right to education. In this historical context, South Sudan is one of the worst places with an 83% of literacy rate. This naturally implies that an enormous number of children are still out of school.

In a historical reality, South Sudanese youth and children have been depressingly affected by an extensive history of armed conflict and inter-ethnic tensions. As a direct result of continuous armed confrontations in many parts of the world, people fear for their lives, and some would resort to seeking safety and security internally and externally. Muggah and Berman (2001) underscore that the local availability of small arms and their unprofessional use has negative impacts such as forced migration of civilians and the decline of the household's critical necessities. This negative impact of wars does not merely affect the education sector, but it also impacts negatively on socio-economic development at family and community levels. Similarly, this has traditionally been the case in South Sudan where over a million ordinary citizens have been displaced internally and externally. As a result of war, displacement is rampant in South Sudan, and it is so desperately deplorable.

In other independent countries around the globe, such internal and external displacements have already happened and are however happening to the effective date. For this reason, most children either missed out on their education or are subjected to getting poor education. Crossing over to the Middle East, the civil war in Syria between 2011 and 2015 displaced about 23 million of innocent civilians, which 7.6 million were internally displaced while 4 million were externally moved as refugees to the neighboring countries of Lebanon, Turkey, and Jordan

(Culbertson & Constant, 2015). This indicates that children who are fondly supposed to be in the school for learning are vulnerable to neglect, exploitation of all forms as well as being confined in violent conflicts. On the other hand, Vaessen et al. (2016) claimed that approximately 400,000 students have missed school in the states of the Greater Upper Nile Region between 2013 and 2015. Indeed, these shocking figures are not new in the war-affected regions, but the concerned governments treat them unconscientiously and ignorantly instead of adequately addressing them as a matter of concern and urgency.

At this point in time, the performance of education has been worsened by the presence of COVID-19 pandemic, which spared no country globally. It is imperative that the social impact of conflict and closure of schools for more than a year due to the COVID-19 pandemic, has kept some learners including teachers away from the learning centers. The complex situation in South Sudan is still unstable with frequent reports on civil unrest resulting from continued tribal revenge wars in a considerable number of villages and states. Moreover, cattle raids and criminal activities on the roads and at the corresponding community areas have posed a great risk and untold suffering. There are now isolated accounts of occupation of schools by warring armies. In notable addition, floods have wantonly destroyed school structures and displaced populations typically confining them to local camps of settlements. The displaced populations are incapable to check-out the land which amounts to food insecurity. Some children have voluntarily stopped attending school due to apparent lack of food and school fees to enthusiastically support their education.

Child soldiers and their families may flee their homes for refuge seeking internally or externally to escape child recruitment. Whereas, other children and their families flee to active military barracks for protection. As conflicts intensify, both learners and their respective families may split apart and displaced. Innocent victims of child soldiers have been forced or lured into armed groups to undoubtedly suffer a broad range of human rights violations and abuses. This additionally includes emphatic denial of right to life, right to not be subjected to sexual violence or other forms of torture, right to education and right to freedom of thought conscience.

Traumatic Incidents and Stressful Routines Encountered by the Learners and School Personnel

As a consistent result of devastating conflicts that involve the loss of lives, possible survivors of conflict and disasters become psychologically traumatized and morally dehumanized. It is an ordinary phenomenon that most of the victims and survivors of wars experience various types of suffering and hardships as a result of the war. According to Muggah and Berman (2001), armed conflict does not only lead to imminent death, but can equally contribute to psychosocial trauma and distressing events to the victims and the eyewitnesses of the brutal atrocities committed during the wars. In most cases, the victims are unarmed innocent civilians including the learners, the teaching force, and the parents who lose their relatives and witness the traumatic experiences during crises.

In this respect, psychological and emotional injuries may be the long-term effects of war; yet historically; they may be the least addressed in practical terms of establishing a civil society and preventing future violence to invariably occur (Lisa, 2012). Substantially, traumatic events in the face of humanitarian emergencies typically tend to be dramatic among the affected populations. It should be mentioned that schools are the only safe havens to protect the school children and the youths from enduring effects of the war as well as rebuilding the lives of shattered societies. Certainly, the psychosocial and emotional effects of conflict do not go away easily until effective and corrective measures and keen interventions are expended to address the educational issues regarding the well beings of the community within the school environment.

On the other hand, the possible survivors of all types of linked emergencies may be hopeless and helpless, and so they may commit suicide or homicide if they are not taken care of. In historical fact, suicide and homicide incidents are some of the common negative impacts of wars and other forms of natural and human-made disasters which can be observed in the school and community settings. In an emergency context, problem-related to loss of lives, the disappearance of people, destruction of property, and human displacements remain physically visible among the victims and the wrongdoers. To see whether such social issues apply to an emergency context, Education Cannot Wait (ECW Strategy, 2018-2021) has pointed out that school attendance and learning activities are detrimentally affected by sexual and gender discrimination as well as psychosocial implications.

On this key point, the disappointing performance of the educational system as a result of perpetual interruption plays a negative role in the learning and professional outcomes. The performance of the educational system is correlated with the better performance of the national economy. When traditionally viewing from the perspective of economic benefits, it could be candidly admitted that conflict and other disaster-related implications could force out young men and women from instantly accessing quality education. In this sense, such frequent allusions may output unskilled manpower that does not meet the present 21st century skills needed in the global labor markets. An alternative explanation is that conflict may lead to long-term consequences such as producing an unqualified labor force. Consequently, implying persistent economic instability, loss of educational structures, loss of teaching force to other high-paying jobs, emigration as well as child labor manipulation takes the lead as negative impressions (Mayai & Hammond, 2014). In this divine essence, I sincerely believe that such a situation may pose an economic threat and hardships to individual and community levels. In this central aspect, the key provision of quality education in the face of crises is not taken seriously by the government and other educational actors as a transformative tool for realizing a social change and economic transformation.

To a larger extent, Mundy and Sarah (2011) carefully observed that when the collapse of the schools and the educational system themselves are destroyed, boys and girls are affected, but the implications can be different for girls. Especially, there tend to be no provision of dignity kits and girls change rooms for girls to keep them in the learning settings. In many conflict situations, the negative consequences of war bear an enormous burden on the national education systems and the school administrations in the wide-ranging implications.

Largely, conflict implications endure a great deal that needs to be strategically planned and implemented with collective commitments. For observable reasons, the armed groups destroy physical infrastructures and the scholastic materials of the schools during the war. By comparison, Cahill (2010) has justly estimated 750,000 more children and youth have intentionally missed their education, either disrupted or missed out entirely on education each year owing to humanitarian disasters. A massive displacement of parents, school children and their teachers may lead to the closure of the schools. Hereafter, progressively reducing the level of enrolment rate of any given war-affected nation.

Given that schools and other learning activities are interrupted gently in the times of crisis, it naturally becomes a concern for parents and guardians to entrust their children in the schools. As a result, this leads to a temporary cease of learning opportunities and interruption of embattled educational programs that are to be implemented. As noted by Cahill (2010), around the world, there are approximately 75 million children out of school and more than half of 40 million people live in conflict-affected fragile states. This is evidenced by the fact that parents keep their children at home to avoid being involved in the conflict especially on their trips to and from the school in order to avoid falling victim to landmines (Cahill, 2010). This points to the fact that long-distance to and from the school in most conflict-prone areas in South Sudan has kept most of the school-going age children at home for security and safety ins and outs.

Despite the lifelong commitment of the government to implement the policy of girls' education nationwide, there are still clear indicators that the policy remains in principle but not in practical aspects. The South Sudan General Education Act (2012) clearly spells out that education should achieve equity and promote gender equality and the promotion of the status of women. As such, this is a clear and well-thought education policy that leads to the accomplishment of girl education if it is adequately implemented and very much evaluated. In essential fact, the implementation of educational policies in South Sudan remains a critical issue because of the lack of political will, lack of resources, and insecurity that has overrun the country. This typically implies that the entire community of the school, as well as the education system of the country, is faced with a lot of perpetual problems, which really need collective attention for that matter. Nevertheless, what remains a big destructive impact on the whole education system of the country is the possible diversion of school resources. In fact, regional segregation is an institutional evident and legitimately discriminatory in visible light of the continuous distribution of educational resources which remains as an overriding concern. For apparent reasons, it may hinder the practical application of education in humanitarian emergencies in the face of crises. In addition, what seems to be a familiar phenomenon in the context of educational services delivery in common is the alteration of collegiate funds to other sectors or for the personal gains of the concerned authority.

Basically, the government stands a great chance of being blamed because of its failure or unwillingness to provide security and other basic needs to the ordinary citizens both in the times of emergency and non-emergency. This creates what is the so-called depravity of public resources, which hinders the distinct possibility of the school to efficiently deliver quality educational services. As might be expected, many educational programs and projects previously earmarked by the government genuinely seem to have not been implemented or delivered in an honest routine. With the cultural and tribal polarization on communities is intact, it has become so disturbing when seeing educational opportunities promptly thrown into a wastepaper basket on the pretext of not working collaboratively in emergency contexts. As local emergency and other related disasters strike, it is the role of each member of South and their respective humanitarian organizations and development parents to pay attention to the educational activities to enable learners be confined in the school sceneries to prevent the happenings of traumatic events.

My point of argument is not just providing education, but making sure that children get quality education in a given educational cycle through to tertiary level. Given the low opinion of national educational achievement rates, this alone is an indicator of low-slung enrolment proportion especially in the developing countries and other war-affected countries such as South Sudan, Sudan, Somalia, and others. On the other hand, educational activities delivered during conflicts and other emergencies are often considered less valuable because of inaccessibility to quality educational services. This fact leads us to believe that the quality of education is always very poor and

Some of the Students of Royal Progressive Academy posing for a picture in the school compound in Tonj South County, Warrap State (Courtesy of 2021)

Pupils from Mario Muor Vision International School posing for a group photo in the school premises in Wau, Western Bahr el Ghazal State (Courtesy of 2021)

One of the best female students with high performance in Senior Four Examinations, from Darling Wisdom Academy, Juba (Courtesy of 2021)

weakens the academic credentials awarded to the workforce. This is in line with the compelling argument put forward by Smith (2009) that some undesirable impacts of armed conflict on education severely limit the access and the quality of instruction being provided at all levels of education.

In marked contrast, Mundy and Sarah (2011) claim that children in conflict zones receive a more imperfect quality education and face greater marginalization in education due to abject poverty, gender, and ethnicity than children in countries not affected by conflict. Typically speaking, the kind of educational services provided at the critical time of crises is often of poor quality, and advocacy for quality educational services should also take the central momentum.

Continuous Occupation of Schools and Destruction of Learning Facilities

Factually, schools are comfort zones for peace during crises. In most rare cases, schools and other educational institutions are often occupied by the armed forces. Apparently, this typically leads to a massive displacement of the civil population in reasonable search of their safety zones and safeguarded environment. Such a huge displacement of the schools has not been a new phenomenon in the active war zones especially when there is a possible outbreak of potential conflict. Mayai and Hammond (2014) stressed that educational facilities may be occupied by armed fighters and this may result in the gradual displacement of civil populations due to unending war, in this way, hindering the operations of educational activities. It has been properly reported in the past few years that some schools in Mapel and Tonj were occupied by the armed forces and turned into army ammunition stores. Hence, enabling them to be non-operational by the concerned school frames.

Some of the students from Peace Secondary School posing for a group photo in Gudele Branch, Juba (Courtesy of 2022)

As a direct result, the international community raised the concern and so the SPLA leadership quickly emptied the store and moved out of the learning institutions in 2005 and 2006 respectively. Similarly, Vaessen et al. (2016) have argued that more than 90 schools all over the country were occupied by the armed forces and people displaced internally during the South Sudanese Civil war. This report could be contradictory since there are no specific schools prominently mentioned in that period between 2013 and 2016 to have been occupied by the armed forces. However, in Central Equatoria, it should be noted that schools were occupied and lived in by the gallant soldiers especially in Mahdi and key Acholi corridors and its surrounding localities. For a certain frame of specific references, however, it might be true that some schools were occupied by the armed forces, but could not reach a number, which is half of schools in the country.

As a practical matter of fact, learning spaces and residential areas are constantly monitored by the United Nations in South Sudan and other education stakeholders which could later alert the government to take any necessary measures. In most cases, the war has left many schools abandoned due to the presence of rebel and government forces that could confront themselves from time to time. Moreover, it is a common practice in fragile states run by weak military governments that concentrated most of the learning institutions willingly suffer from constant attacks by the fighting forces. Indeed, this has unfortunately happened in some countries, which have been invariably involved in military confrontations including South Sudan.

Educational facility means any building used predominantly for educational purposes in which a school is located and a proper course of instructions is offered that has been approved and licensed by a state educational agency. Primarily, an apparent lack of secure facilities intentionally limits the unique ability of a student to realistically achieve various learning and extra curricula activities. This is because of a lack of facilities has a negative impact on a prospective teachers' job satisfaction, which subtly undermines their possible motivation to teach correctly.

In an educational reality, good and adequate learning facilities positively influence their creative thinking to perform well in learning process and comprehensive examination. Henceforth, this may improve students' academic achievement and professional inclination. On the other hand, poor infrastructure affects students learning abilities and likewise to teachers' unique ability to teach. It has been justly observed in different learning situations that poor infrastructure in schools can also be seen in learners' dropout rates and low-teachers' retention rates. Illustratively, poor building conditions may include leaking and foul-smelling toilets, dirty cafeterias, broken furniture, classrooms that are too hot or cold, neglected walls and plaster falling off ceilings.

In brilliant light of this assured destruction of learning facilities, it is an overbearing datum that most of the learning institutions across the different conflict-affected states could often fall victims. In addition, Samman et al. (2018) have triumphantly pointed out that, in many crises, attacks are targeted on schools or schools are used by the militaries and this restricts access to schooling by teachers and learners. At the global level, the comparative study conducted in Yemen by the United Nations Children's Fund (UNICEF, 2018c) indicated that in March 2018 about 2,500 schools were reported to have been used by armed forces while 66% were destroyed by violence, yet 27% were closed down with 7% occupied by displaced persons (as cited in Samman et al., 2018). Though there are no more available data to support this claim, it should be noted that conflicts fought within the same country turn out to be upsetting in nature. As a result, this affects learning institutions as opponent forces compete to take advantage and control more territories in order to establish rapport with the inhabiting communities.

In direct comparison, in Nigeria for instance, Tukur (2017) and Onuoha et al. (2018) have contended that conflicts between the government and Boko Haram insurgency have led to the death of some 2,295 teachers and the destruction of more than 1,400 schools (as cited in Samman et al., 2018). Outwardly, this is not a social illusion in the civil war in Nigeria as kidnapping and abducting of learners and teachers have been the order of the day. Following the outbreak of the conflict in those regions of Nigeria where Boko Haram has been operating, their main activities have been concentrated fiercely to destroy physical school facilities and destruction of human lives.

On the contrary, rapes and major sexual exploitation have been reported in Uganda, typically following the long-drawn-out war led by Joseph Kony, a notorious leader of the Lord Resistance Army (LRA) in the western and eastern part of Uganda. In many respects, Samman et al. (2018) flatly put it that both girls and women, in most cases, could be stranded in conflict and they suffer from fundamental inequalities, violence, and even trafficking abuses. As such, this typically limits their active participation in the decision-making processes as well as in the socio-economic development of the country. This is a negative precedence since abduction and raping of school girls is some major war crimes which ought to solve through the respect of international and domestic laws.

Rapid Increased Cases of Rape and Sexual Exploitation

Rape and sexual harassment have been evidenced as major problems facing girls' education throughout the conflict situations. Because of war, women and girls are exposed to grave sexual abuses by men in uniform and other war criminals in the conflict-affected areas. Given the historical fact that women are part of the vulnerable groups that cannot defend themselves, they end up, with intolerance of sexual exploitation. Mundy and Sarah (2011) have pointed out that rape, and sexual harassment is apparently used as primary weapons of war. For instance, following the direct confrontation of government and rebel forces in Juba in 2016, cases of rape and sexual violence by armed men against women and girls were reported at Jebel checkpoints and other areas across the country. Though both sides continue to steadfastly deny these disturbing and prevalent facts, there is clear evidence on the moral ground to sufficiently prove these specific cases of rape to a larger extent.

Categorically, both nationals and expatriates were reported as victims of rapes by government forces at Terrain Hotel, the suburban area of Juba Town. However, the prime suspects were promptly arrested and were arraigned before the local court of law. Nevertheless, the identified victims complained of likely culprits not being persecuted by the competent court of law. By the time of publishing this book, the details of the official persecution were not released to prove to the general public whether the rule of law took its course or not. As a result of such inhuman acts against girls, most of the parents restrict their daughter not to continue with their studies due to the fear of the unknown. More recent analyses have correctly pointed out those parents do not allow their daughters to attend school for the fear that their daughters would be victims of violence and especially sexual vehemence, either in the school itself or even on route to it (Mundy and Sarah, 2011). On this consistent basis, I believe that throughout the conflict situations, girls are vulnerable to sexual abuse and other forms of sexual exploitation on their way to and from the school.

Rape and sexual exploitation remain the critical violation of the rights of girls and women across the country. Both rape and sexual harassment have been observed as the most underreported crime in South Sudan and elsewhere in the fragile states. Due to low education and awareness raising campaigns across the country, significant changes to adequately protect women and girls have not improved the treatment of sexual assault victims in the forgoing decades. However, there is a lesser impact of reforms, though concerted efforts were put by different women activists to improve the legal, mental health, medical, and victim service systems. The treatment of victims in the criminal justice system has been interrogated, though a handful of laws have been passed to protect rape victims in the courts.

From the context of EiE, widespread insecurity has been widely cited as an obstacle to girl education nationally and globally. Given such massive obstacles to girl education, it is the one and only undertaking of the EiE to make sure that girl education be given a huge pat so that they equally participate in the educational activities alongside the boys. Furthermore, the long-distance to school is also a major concern for parents who send their daughters to schools located far away from their homes. These emotional disturbances and social implications continue to exist and bear serious consequences on the education of girls at their homes. In fact, this continues to be a proven fact that makes their access to schooling lower than that for boys. For instance, some schools in South Sudan are located at a distance of more than 10 kilometers and this makes it difficult for girls to move to and from the school safely during emergency situations. Thus, their educational opportunities are limited, making girls' enrolment rate less compared to that of boys. This is indeed a great obstacle to girl schooling countrywide, and this gently encourages forced marriage and early pregnancies among the school age-going girls.

Rampant Insecurity and Learning Disenfranchisement Rampant

Security for both humans and material resources remains one of the major concerns for everyone, especially in the event that insecurity becomes rampant. However, the issue of security and safety for learners, teachers, and parents is equally threatened especially in the time of crises. During an emergency context, insecurity becomes one of the biggest threats to schooling and its surrounding areas. For instance, according to South Sudan Education Cluster (2014, as cited in Mayai, & Hammond, 2014), approximately 12, 000 learners in the Greater Upper Nile Region (Upper Nile State, Jonglei State, and Unity State) were forced out of schools due to widespread insecurity and lack of educational resources. The spread of economic insecurity across different learning environments is one of the noticeable challenges facing education in a time of humanitarian emergencies. The presence of armed men and women in the neighborhood of the school community threatens the security and safety of the learners, teachers, and other school personnel.

In reality within the emergency context, it should be mentioned that educational activities are gaining less momentum of socio-economic improvement and also in line with the unique application of EiE. This is coupled by a lack of sensitization of the school communities at the grassroots levels in relation to the importance of education during an emergency crisis. It is imperative that the primary goal of education in common is to serve the primary needs of the national socio-economic development of a given country. However, much of the expectations of the ordinary citizens have never been met given the necessity to provide education for all. Nonetheless, in my view, the leadership of the young nation is not preparing and equipping the youths and school children with relevant knowledge and skills that can enable them to play effective roles in the development of their nation.

From the security standpoint, pastoral education during crisis could also add a practical advantage to the improvement and adherence to national security laws that safeguard the country. Indeed, mobile schooling during crises could be one of the educational realities in which the common citizen could think of as alternative solutions. As McEvoy & LeBrun (2010) put it, security is threatened due to the continuous availability of firearms in the hands of civilians, and their beliefs in the power of their guns could terribly encourage the flourish of conflict.

In this respect, this calls for the government to prevent the civilians from candidly owning guns so that the lives of the school personnel are not threatened. In most conflict-prone nation-states including South Sudan, the proliferation of small arms in the hands of individuals have created insecurity, hence threatening the performance of the education system. In addition, propagation of small arms in the hands of unarmed youths have encouraged cattle rustling in which the insecurity apparatus keeps on multiplying damagingly, and this poses a greater risk to the respective communities in which schools are located. Henceforth, creating fear for the unknown to the lives of innocent learners, school community and their property.

In a presentable reputable fact, economic insecurity impedes schooling activities which may lead to shutting down of schools and prevents the government and other education actors from reopening schools. Not only closing down learning centers, it also causes mental related health issues to learners and teachers which are credibly be inform of economic depression, low self-esteem and socio-economic anxieties. Indeed, insecurity in one way or the other, is a contributing factor to eating and sleeping disorders among the members of the school community. In the context of South Sudan, insecurity has drastically exacerbated the performance of the national education sector at all levels of education. To a larger extent, both students, teachers and the government are being frustrated and disappointed in multiple times. Hence, leading to worst educational wastage across the country. In light of this reality check, insecurity situation in the country naturally prompts all local people to put forward extraordinary measures to combat it before it progressively worsens human lives and destroys their property.

Common Occurrence of Interethnic Tensions and Inter-Communal Conflicts

Speaking in reference to tribal wars fought in South Sudan, schools are frequently threatened and sometimes learners and the school personnel are deliberately killed and intimidated at gun points. This has made life hard for their safety and security, consequently disrupting teaching and learning activities as scheduled. The ongoing wars fought along ethnic lines, communities have been socially at odds and culturally divided in many respects. It has become cautionary that tribesmen pay political and military allegiances to their tribal leaders either in government or in opposing sides to wage wars. In fact, many lives have been lost and property destroyed simply because of lack of education at the peripheries.

Ethnic conflict occurs between ethnic groups to achieve political or economic goals, whereas national conflict involves one or more groups striving for sovereignty. Intercommunal conflict is the term used to describe conflict that occurs between competing groups within a state. It may arise over disputes concerning access to scarce resources, social eccentricities, or politically connected to search for power. In fact, such endless conflicts have led to violent warfare among diverse ethnic communities across the country. In addition, ethnic conflicts have very direct effects far beyond their midpoints. For example, these include refugee flows, internal displacement, regional instability, economic failures, environmental disasters, diffusion and spillover effects, and conditions favorable to organized crime and terrorism. For instance, most of communal conflicts in South Sudan affect the schooling in one way or the other. Despite the widespread of these communal conflicts, it is still one of the core objectives of the Government is to ensure the line bureaucracies and line ministries should be close to the members of the community and provide a forum where local people can dialogue among themselves to develop their local communities.

The essence of conceiving the idea to educate people has been a past due notion to use as a standpoint to get rid of illiteracy and change the mindsets of the armed youth, once and for all. In this respect, continuity of the learning activities is something that can be maintained when war has started. In this context, an extensive history of interethnic conflict in South Sudan has remained the phenomenal practice in the antiquity of South Sudan. So, this has forced most children to be no longer interested to attend school due to fear of their lives and victimization. In terms of employment opportunities, many employees could lose their jobs if the schools are not operational. This solely causes socio-economic gaps in the family income of those affected.

Muggah and Berman (2001) have observed that armed conflict causes unemployment and inequality due to the widespread of handguns. This is a genuine point in the sense that South Sudanese conflicts are supervened due to a lack of national consensus and trust among the diverse ethnic communities. At some point, this is also coupled with limited power-sharing and unequal allocation of national and public resources, gender discrimination in all forms, and others. In the context of South Sudan, constitutional and educational policies established by the day-to-day leadership of the country are not implemented as desired and expected by the common people. As such, this has manifested itself in the polarization of tribes against one another rather than having a plurality of people in support of the constituted educational policies. However, educational service delivery seems to have been based on the separatist and isolated policy adopted illegally by the South Sudanese local communities. For instance, a teacher who hails from another region does not stand a chance of being employed in the schools in which they do not maintain originality of the location. This is because the individualized occupation and social segregations at the community level take superiority over other tribes.

From the global perspective, Bekerman & Zembylas (2012) pointed out that separatist policies are most visible in educational arrangements fully practiced by the Palestinian and the Jewish communities. In principle, South Sudan does not encourage the application of separatist policies, but some elements of discrimination of ethnicities are noticeable in some administrations of learning institutions. Such adamant policies are standard in practice and are obviously encouraged by the wars being fought on the basis of tribal allegiances and regional and political affiliations. In this sense, education is a valid and reliable tool that can transform the cultural and societal values, which is seen to be encouraging conflicts in some ways. For instance, in some communities, most of the young men with marked foreheads who have under no circumstances been to school do not value education at all. As follows, they are likely to cause violence within their respective communities and also with their neighbors.

At this point in time, these cultural practices are outlived and assume no importance in modern societies where education has taken a lead in transforming people's lives, cultures, and futures as far as reflecting on the importance of education is concerned. On the same note, marking faces and some parts of the body as tribal symbols, which are widely practiced among Dinka, Nuer, Shilluk, Murle or Mundari tribes. Symbolically, these represent societal symbols which can portray one's cultural importance and social significance. Though such cultural or tribal marks possess symbolic importance in their respective neighborhoods, it has been noted in the previous years during the conflict that people have been identified on the basis of their marks and were victimized. With education, such negative cultures could be eliminated since some of them accept harmful implications while others characterize a sign of defeatist attitudes. This would foster unity in a manner that all South Sudanese would be able to identify themselves on the basis of patriotic citizens to promote an agenda of one country.

In comparison, this is invariably noticeable in the social, political, and economic spheres of life in South Sudan, although it is legally unpermitted and practically encouraged. With the onset of conflict polarizing the ordinary citizens along ethnic lines, it is observed that some tribes are too harsh to others. They may implement geographical discrimination as a tool to revenge their political disappointment and social frustrations. For instance, the report documents indicate varied opinions on the prevalence of enforced disappearances, torture, rape, and conflict-related intimate violence and the forced recruitment of child soldiers throughout the country. In fact, significant human rights abuse such as reports of extrajudicial and arbitrary killings, cases of cruel, inhuman and degrading treatment by reportedly rogue elements of the security apparatus, especially in conflict zones. Likewise, harsh and life-threatening prison conditions and serious problems with politicization are seemingly intact.

Though such discrimination was not there before, some scholars have written in the past years, clearly pointed out diverse opinions in disgust in light of a serious divergence of tribes. It is plainly conspicuous on the grounds that a self-fulfilling prophecy is being advanced by some South Sudanese communities and particularly tribally-aligned scholars. Indeed, this has created wider social and cultural divides among different ethnic groups in South Sudan. Summing it up altogether, this can create a negative boldness to the schooling activities and professional obligations, despite socio-economic efforts to build vibrant and educated South Sudanese communities.

An Unexpected Increase of Street Children & Orphans

Due to continuous civil wars besetting South Sudan for decades, many children have left the schools and their respective homes and ended up on the street looking for essential needs for survival. In the streets of almost all the towns in the Republic of South Sudan, thousands of street children have been displaced involuntarily as beggars or homeless. Without wars being fought, public resources spent on war mercenaries on both sides of the conflict would have definitely been used to establish schools and other vocational training centers to absorb these hopeless street children. Astonishingly, most of the street children and adults in their early twenties are believed to be former fighters who are disappointed in one way or the other, because of some reasons attached to their respective military leaderships in both sides of the conflict.

To a larger extent, the street or homeless children have the odds stacked against them across the country. They are exposed to maximal elements of suffering with an uncertain supply of food and medical supplies. They are likely to miss out on education and parental care while others are at high risk of suffering from drug addiction, exploitation abuse and emergency related illnesses. A single child alone on the streets is especially vulnerable to death and mental disorder. Hence, chances for a child to die from parental carelessness and lack of access to basic education are very high and emotionally overwhelming.

In South Sudan, the major causes for children to take to the streets are poverty, lack of educational opportunities and vast families. In addition, limited access to basic social services, breakdown of basic family structures, and the shift from traditional values that tend to be money-oriented have discriminated children against the government efforts to educate them. On the other hand, those boys who turn out to be night robbers, as well as those who are terrorizing innocent lives in different residential and suburban areas, are among learners who should have been in the school if it was not for the outbreak of civil war in South Sudan. Suspiciously, some of the unknown gunmen and women operating in Juba and other major towns in South Sudan are perceived to be among those street adults. It could be admitted that most of them have no basic education, and in this sense, they might collaborate with some culprits to conduct criminal activities at night or during the day in isolated areas for survival.

Low Morale in the Teaching Profession

The teaching profession is the least desired field for old and emerging young professionals due to poor remunerations and lack of psychological feature and intended services. Perceptibly, there are numerous causes of low teacher morale in the school setting. Among these roots include poor status in the community, poor and relative salaries to other professions, poor student behavior, excessive workload, poor leadership, and appalling working conditions. These causes of low morale in the teaching profession are first and foremost, responsible for teacher turnover, which can negatively impact the whole public education system.

In addition, teacher low morale breeds a reduction in productivity and academic performance on the side of the learners. It is presumptuous below par, in a sense that when teachers maintain low morale, they are less eager to give their best, which leads to poor quality work or assignments that are not turned in on time. This has given a no-return room for unqualified ones to fill and sanctify the teaching profession. This is because teaching remains the lowest valued profession in South Sudan and perhaps in other parts of the world due to modest pay and coupled with non-existing compensations. In South Sudan, budget difficulty remains the leading factor to low teacher morale which is triggered by stagnant pay. Though teaching is still being considered a noble profession, it is clear that the field is being deserted by qualified manpower. As a result, highly motivated teachers support children to learn best through a passionate and skilled instruction.

Often what frustrates teachers the most is the perception that their voice is not heard in public discussions about educational issues which hinder the performance of the education system. Teachers feel to be part and parcel of positive social change in the communities. In light of this, they should be empowered to be leaders in and out of the school and contributing members of education policy discussions. Given these facts, educational activities in the face of crises are worsened; henceforward, poor cultural standards override the national education system. It is imperative to note that teaching as a profession is about inspiring and motivating students to achieve and exceed their potentials.

Furthermore, the teaching profession is jeopardized by the ongoing crises since the national resources are sometimes diverted to security in the name of protecting the national territories and people. These implications tell us that much of the annual budget of the country is largely consumed by the defense and national security sectors in case of a man-made disaster. However, many teachers have not devoted their lives to inspire and empower their students to achieve tremendous things and to be good human beings. In this essence, it is clear that the exclusion of awareness-raising components in relation to the importance of teacher education during any crisis remains a community inevitability to be desired.

Viewing it strategically from the instructional-based approach, teaching and learning activities during crises are crucially important and should be time-bound. This is because new knowledge and skills are delivered by the learned or teachers and digested by the learners. In this way, it enhances the high-quality academic performance on the side of the students and continuity of the learning in a given school academic year calendar. Hence improving the quality of education and pedagogical standards at the national and individual levels. However, poor teacher morale can negatively affect student achievement and performance. It is imperative that high teacher morale can boost student performance, in this way, improving the learning outcomes. In the same way, students who maintain higher morale are more likely to enjoy school, be successful, and have a positive view of education.

As far as teaching profession is concerned, the core of teaching consists of four basic values like dignity, truthfulness, fairness, responsibility and academic freedom. Honesty with oneself and others and mutual respect in all the chains of communication are a basic aspect of teacher's work. It is intellectually commanding that teachers make up the most leading part of the school and spend the most time with students. As such, an inspired teacher always has compassion for their students, understanding of their students' personal lives, and appreciation for their academic goals and achievements. Teachers are role models for children to be positive who encourage them to reach their desired stars. If the school system wants to employ and retain best teachers to perform at the highest level, they must feel satisfied with their jobs.

Overall, the best way to improve the education system is to strategize on the teaching force, the learning materials and facilities. It is also imperative the security and safety of physical and human materials are highly warranted and uninterruptedly maintained. In addition, the recruitment of qualified and motivated teachers can help improve the face of the teaching profession at all levels of education. In this perspective, a qualified teaching force possesses knowledge in relation to content, learners' abilities, lesson preparation, and learning environment. Henceforth, learners' diversity, effective management of the classroom, the quality-based assessment remains the key performance-based components. In order to have qualified teachers on board, it is domineering that recruitments should be transparent and non-partisan so that diversity and equity of teaching force is adequately reflected in the staffing recruitment and deployment process.

PART FOUR

Considering Education as a Shared Responsibility

The Stance of the Government in Considerable Time of Crises

The key roles of the Government in the specific provision of EiE remains exclusively an outstanding commitment and mandatory factor to be exercised legally and objectively. Given the fact that the government in common is the sole provider of key services, it should be noted that education is one of the national programs to be given closer attention in all emergency and no-emergency backgrounds. No practical matter where and how the emergency situations strike, it is significant to acknowledge that the responsibilities solely remain with the government to take the lead to provide a conducive learning and non-threatening environment.

To contemplate in a more democratic stand and realistic approach regarding the leading role of the government, the solitary response would correctly be that the social responsibilities of government are manifold. Most importantly, the government should typically provide and guarantee adequate security both to the learners, teachers, university instructors, and educational laborers at all levels of education. Secondly, it is still a known charge of the government to protect the physical assets from being carefully manipulated or damaged by armed forces or other criminals operating within or outside the political and social vacuums. Finally, this is all about keeping people safe and adequately protecting their unique property by all costs and means.

In light of this responsibility, the government is obliged to provide affordable and accessible educational opportunities during humanitarian crises. Provision of education should not be discriminatory, but it ought to ensure that all learners have equal and unhindered access to learning opportunities. Providing learners with equal and unhindered access to educational opportunities regardless of their respective tribes, regions or political affiliations is a collective responsibility for all citizens. This is because the government in any given nation-state is ostensibly the sole provider of all fundamental services including maximum security to its citizens. Nonetheless, there are some unique situations where the government fails to execute its apparent and usual responsibilities. This raises many doubts and questions from individuals who may expect major interventions that characterize the role of the government in times of crisis. The failure of the government to provide equal educational opportunities during crises may generate many answers than questions from like-minded people who love to solve critical educational issues during an emergency context.

As emergency strikes, the government and the partners take the lead to identify the necessities on the ground including human and materials resources. As soon as the areas of need are spotlighted, the most important thing is to provide maximum security to protect the human and material resources from being used or damaged by the confronting forces. This could create an enabling learning environment for learners, teachers, parents and other educational laborers. Alternatively, in protecting the school community, the security and safety of the surrounding residential areas where learners come from, could also be guaranteed within and outside the school premises. This encourages trust among the longtime residents to support the remarkable continuity of learning activities in a friendly, conducive, and inclusive learning environment. Equally important, security and access to educational facilities and resources remain the key issue that needs to be critically ministered to with an open mind. Since there is a situation that may predict and senses danger, it is an integral role for the government to coordinate the security of both human and material resources within and outside the school setting.

Noticeably, learning institutions become apparently inaccessible especially when the prevailing situation naturally tends to threaten human lives. As it happens, security is a desirable and demand for everyone including the school children and the youth. During an emergency, the security of people and particularly school children remains an issue of concern to parents, guardians, and all community members. From a security-wise, this depends upon confidence-building among the school children, parents and the well-wishers to be ensured so as to create better working conditions.

Not to mention, the government should employ emergency and preparedness planning strategies to stabilize the negative collisions, which may happen or expect to take place as a result of the catastrophes. According to Mundry and Sarah (2011), investing in education before an emergency unfolds is more cost-effective than waiting until an emergency develops unexpectedly. This entails that acting swiftly when emergencies strike is far better than waiting for crisis to start. With humanitarian emergency knocking at the country's doorsteps, many scholars and policy actors have always emphasized preparedness and planning as the first step to be taken in case of any emergency that may strike.

Likewise, the government should ensure educational activities should go uninterrupted during and after the conflict. This means that if the educational programs are maintained, then the comparative safety of the school children and other personnel is maximally assured. Furthermore, Smith (2009) believes that education offers protection and other support to the learners during emergencies, post-conflict periods, and in a state of fragility. By carefully putting schools in an undisrupted state-run commitment, it can encourage the educational aims to flourish, therefore leading to the continuity and completion of a given educational cycle by learners.

Consistently, it is a well-known fact today that schools continue to be the safe havens during any crisis because the learners and teachers are confined in the school setting. Hence, this reduces the risk of being knowingly exposed to the hostile environment of social and armed threats, intimidation, and other forms of criminal activities. This direct observation was also put forward by Samman et al. (2018) that quality education is a fundamental human right and can provide a pathway for social development that encourages fairness, equality, and justice for all. This gentle hint at the accomplished fact that the government should provide a conducive and supportive learning environment that can support the physical safety, moral and psychological development of learners.

Along comparable lines of paramount importance, major educational activities and programs cannot be implemented without funds made available by the government to the relevant state ministries, education actors and the concerned school authority to deliver vital educational activities. This demands the government to increase the educational budget and gently release educational funds in a timely and proactive manner. For this specific purpose, it is meant to counteract the potential impacts that might be intentionally inflicted on human and material resources in the areas of its jurisdiction. In other words, the government should avail enough funds and initiate other educational programs and projects in submission to implementing its educational policies in a manner expected by the citizens in time of crisis. This mandatory binder calls for the government to expend financial commitments by all possibilities to make sure that any penny is devoted to the education sector.

Since it is efficiently the government's social responsibility to fund educational activities, it is important that more funding is needed to complement the already existing services. Releasing more educational resources means adequately compensating for the damage that might have been caused by the crises. In addition, these replicative efforts are meant to extricate educational challenges during emergencies and avoid potential negative implications on the modern education system, individuals, community, and at national levels. In the event where some levels of collateral damages are reported in the school community, it requires some needs assessments to be conducted collectively. This will help the educational planners to ascertain the level of destruction and areas of necessities, which necessitate an immediate response. This means that the government ought to provide an overall assessment exercise to establish the level of damage caused by the humanitarian crises and to recommend the necessary and appropriate course actions to be taken instantly.

Equally important, the objective of an accurate assessment of extensive damage is typically meant to identify how many learning spaces and teaching force is needed based on assessment, analysis and precisely targeting informed decisions. Although there is no undeviating relationship between class sizes and learning outcomes, greater gains could be made elsewhere in light of teacher training to put forward an ideal minimum standard of teacher preparation. Conversely, this decision needs to be based on factors which require immediate attention as correlated to the context and phases of conflicts. These may typically include the teacher caseload, passionate intensities of risk, and potential vulnerability of learners and teachers. To make it sustainable enough, the assessment should be a continuous process and seek multi-layered participants of diverse organizations and line ministries to uniquely identify multiple areas of needs like health, education, child protection, food security and livelihood. The findings of such many-sided assessments may give the government an idea about the situation on the ground regarding the areas of strategic interventions.

On the same note, building trust among the people from all works of life provides a safe and non-threatening environment that encourages mutual cooperation and peaceful coexistence within the school and its surroundings. Put differently, this guarantees girls an access to education and continue with their schooling during an emergency situation. This hint at the reality that the safety of girls and women is properly safeguarded from being victims of unprovoked assaults, rape, attempted murder, and other forms of violence directed to them by the armed forces. Conversely, because of the fact that women and girls remain the major targets during emergencies because of their vulnerabilities in society, there is a need to provide and strengthen the laws that can protect them and their physical assets. As such, the implementation of girl education during the humanitarian emergency and non-emergency crises is a critical step forward, particularly in the context of achieving a high rate of female literacy rates at the national level.

Likewise, Samman et al. (2018) argue that supporting girls during the crisis and hostile situations should be based on targeted investments that are inclusive to access to education at all levels of learning. In South Sudan in particular and other war-affected regions in general, such targeted investments are of limited applications simply because no any line departments and administrative assignments seem to be showing care and concerns about the education of girls and women in non-emergency and emergency contexts.

Hence, providing affordable education, security, and convenient learning spaces for girls in times of crisis are a worthwhile goal to be enthusiastically supported in a forward-thinking lens and to be protected at all costs. In order to make girls' education more viable and sustainable, it is the role of the government to plan, design, and execute targeted educational activities during crises. As a matter of fact, such focused affirmative deeds for girls may include the provision of scholarships, free education and reduction of tuition fees at all levels of education. Though such directed investments would not benefit all dear girls and women, it is sensible for the few to benefit from such appealing educational opportunities.

On the other hand, the government should adhere to its existing policy commitments to be efficiently implemented in the letter and spirit. Revitalizing and strengthening the prevailing educational policies may also include any accessible legal instruments that support girl education across South Sudan. In this respect, Education Cannot Wait (ECW; 2018-2021) in its ECW Strategy paper accentuates that gender equality in the school settings can be improved by enabling a stable environment where teachers are morally and financially supported. Moreover, this sounds reasonable if educational policies are practically implemented, scholastic materials provided, and best instructional practices are adequately availed especially to the vulnerable learners and children with mild disabilities.

Naturally, drawing it from this confirmatory reality, support for girl education represents not to be a waste of resources as many local communities assume, but it is about scaling up the literacy and numeracy improvement and enrolment rates of girls at all levels of education. By doing so, it adequately provides a favorable environment that encourages the promotion of quality education for all girls as well as improving gender equality in the places of work throughout the country. In light of this, Cahill (2010) stresses enough the specific need to uniquely design and properly implement specific plans to avoid the exploitation of girls and young women in the wake of emergencies. Traditionally, given the vulnerability of female learners during crises, the learning institutions should be empowered with legal instruments meant to protect susceptible learners, and more especially girls in all learning institutions.

More importantly, awareness-raising campaigns at the grassroots levels in an effort to sensitize the communities about the provision of quality educational services to the learners during an emergency context need to be intensified. For specific straightforward reasons, EiE in any situation has ever been given due attention by some communities in South Sudan in particular and the other least developed countries in general. This is attributed to a lack of civic awareness campaigns and coupled with a lack of institutional will to fully inform the communities about the importance of education not only in emergency situations, but also in all non-emergency contexts. To do this effectively, it calls upon the government to employ some proactive measures such as sending constitutional post holders like members of parliament and other influential and legitimate post holders to enlighten and sensitize the masses about the importance of Education in Emergencies.

More concerted efforts are needed in areas of mass education campaigns so that all South Sudanese communities are sophisticated about the importance of girl education since educating a girl implies improvingly her life and that of her family. However, the claim that public awareness campaigns be intensified is the least effective aspect per now, and this is not satisfactory and sustainable in the watch of the majority of the wider composition of responsible citizenship. This is because affirmative practices aimed at minimizing gender discrimination and socio-economic exclusion to ensure equal gender representation in all legal and institutional spheres of life has not helped to scale up educational prospects in the face of crises.

Though in some social contexts where traditional cultural practices such as forced marriage remain powerful, it is true to some extent that education can help them to adjust for the common good for all the people. In this background, Smith (2009) typically considers that education is the means of transmitting cultural and societal values from one generation to another with regards to discouraging negative stereotypes which may cause conflict as well as dispensing positive attitudes that cannot condone conflict. In some cultural contexts, community norms with discriminative cultures have already added negative impressions on girl education, hence limiting gender equity in the education sector.

On the different commitments, the local communities should be mobilized, sensitized, and fully involved in the education matters. This in common is because there is always a close relationship between educational institutions and the prominent members of the communities in which they are intentionally set to typically operate. In this note, typically involving the communities in the selection of the most appropriate response and favorable strategies can start with monitoring the learning and teaching activities in a given school environment. To a considerate emphasis, this additionally includes taking into consideration the issue of gender sensitivity and social inclusiveness.

In notable addition, the government should review and re-examine the education system and policy action plans so as to adopt the desirable and affordable curriculum to the public. Since the government implements its national agenda through its legalized bureaucracies, it is prudent for the national government to support and promptly initiate workshops, seminars, and other appealing public rallies. These social activities should be typically organized and implemented in community resource centers to help people cope with the prevailing situations. As a matter of fact, conducting meaningful workshops and seminars meant to enlighten the general public about the development of emergency and how to be protected from insecurity remains an underpinning feature to reduce fear and panic for the populace.

In many respects, helping communities with adorable psychosocial support services is a worth remarkable backing for that matter. In an effort to provide psychological and psychosocial support services to the affected individuals, what is more, to bear in mind is the training of the stakeholders who can give counseling services in a variety of ways. To begin with, it is necessary for the trained social and case workers to identify the affected individuals to counsel, and reintegrate them into the community comfort. This is what Lisa (2012) suggests to obtain the economic necessity to empower social workers, competent counselors, comparative psychologists, and other service providers to deal with survivors of suicide, conflicts, and justifiable homicide. In this setting, it is significant for the government and other service providers to train the professionals and social workers on matters related to counseling the potential victims and the wider affected communities. This can also help the victims to recover from the psychological effects of wars and other naturally occurring pandemic infections. This can also be cost effective since the affected learners and teachers are returned to the school setting to undoubtedly continue with their normal learning and teaching activities.

As far as education is genuinely concerned, it is the duty of the government forces on one hand, and the rebel forces, on the other, to intervene whenever necessary to demobilize and disarm child soldiers during wartime. It is equally significant to disassociate warlords and ex-soldiers from armed forces and reintegrate them into their respective communities could make a meaningful transition to civilian life. In all its emphasis and importance, education can also save lives by protecting victims against human exploitation and potential body harm, including the recruitment of children into armed groups, sexual exploitation and gender-based violence. In my opinion, such interventions for child soldiers, school children, and the youth may create a broader social-based understanding of the strategic modalities to address the immediate needs through demobilizing, disarming, and reintegrating them into their respective communities. By doing so, children and youth will gain resilient tendencies, which will help them to build their educational capacities and the socio-economic fabric of their respective families.

From the favorable view of effective management, it is also the role of the government to train teachers in robust teaching pedagogies and school administrators in management and outstanding leadership skills. This implies that emergency situations require strong school leadership to meditate on key issues to do with the planning of the day-to-day management of the school affairs based on the prevailing situations. After all, the local school administrators and teachers should possess a variety of proficiencies and skills such as communication, decision-making, and problem-solving skills. It is imperative that the government avails enough funds to cater for the proper training of teachers and school leaders to develop the capacity of the teaching force in order to appreciate a quality education system.

The bottom line reality is that quality education represents a social issue of concern to everyone who wish their children to perform well academically and professionally. As humanitarian emergencies undoubtedly continue to deepen, it does not mean that quality education should not be given an equal reflection. However, it is the committed, motivated, and qualified teachers who influence the delivery of quality educational services during emergencies. In other contexts, learning institutions may be operating during the crisis, but the quality of knowledge being delivered tends to be very poor and South Sudan is not an exception to that element.

Furthermore, it is still the responsibility of the government to ensure that the exclusive content being delivered to the learners during emergency situations is of good quality that can grant one to get a job. This is complemented with the continuation of learning at all levels of education right from the nursery, primary, secondary and tertiary levels. It has become a familiar phenomenon that when crises strike, learning institutions are either encouraged to cease activity or suspend activities indefinitely. This is against the right of access to learning opportunities and the necessity of EiE in all hostile educational situations. In this extensive background, it is the title role of the government to keep the balance and check in the context of efficiently delivering quality educational services to the disadvantaged populations. In so far, this is an imperative attitude to improve the accountability measures in the school settings.

On the other hand, the delivery of knowledge and skills to the learners does not happen out of the blue, but it looks for trained teachers to do the job well. Because of a lack of trained manpower in the teaching profession, the quality of the graduates whether at secondary or university levels has always been very poor. For this reason, it is crucial for the government to recruit and train qualified teachers based on equal representation of demographic and geographic compositions of all the tribes in South Sudan and deployed them across the country. This is because the concept of quality education is pivotal in application since it has some bearings on the improvement of people's lives in terms of meaningfully improving socio-economic development and advancing technological outlooks.

Since the beginning of the previous and current conflicts, which have been fought on the basis of ethnic and provincial dimensions, it has remained a worrying situation because unity among the citizens is jeopardized. Consequently, the development of human and material resources is undermined at the national and state levels. Smith (2009) earnestly advises that in the face of conflict or post-conflict situations, there is a need to select a sufficient number of female and male teachers from diverse backgrounds to provide adequate learning opportunities to students of divergent ethnic groups. In this spirit, carefully selecting a sufficient number of male and female teachers from diverse backgrounds to provide learning opportunities to students of different ethnic groups may minimize the negative perceptions among people that the war is a tribal conflict, which seems to be fought along ethnic lines.

Moreover, the transparent selection and intensive training of teachers also need to be augmented with the key provision of intrinsic and extrinsic motivations. This means that teachers need to be enthusiastically supported with adequate motivation, reasonable accommodations, and transportations to and from homes, social and medical-related insurances. Though people have always emphasized that teachers need to be trained on jobs, it should be mentioned that most teachers in South Sudan possess desired professional qualifications. They also possess considerate teaching experiences that can enable them to reasonably manage and contain the delivery of quality educational services during emergencies. Genuinely, teachers are lacking psychological feature packages in terms of training opportunities and other tangible enticements.

As a direct result of low pay, the meager remuneration has led to low-slung morale among teachers at all appropriate levels of education. However, this is one of the reasons in which the majority of the teaching force is deserting the teaching profession for green pastures outside their principal occupation. Fittingly, Smith (2009) has maintained that teachers need to be typically deployed and offered enough incentives to gently encourage their active participation in the delivery of quality education during emergency situations. By apt comparison, Fullan (2016) accentuates the importance of workstation conditions that *"professionally rewarding workplace conditions attract and retain good people" (p. 97)*. This means that qualified individuals are attracted by the key provision of better work conditions and services. On the odd occasion, this alone ensures quality delivery of educational services to the people, despite the ongoing crises. In practical terms of collaboration, the government in partnership with education and development actors should provide health facilities to be used by the learners and the school workforces in the respective schools. As humanitarian crises unfold, health issues arise, and this puts the lives of school children at risk, if urgent interventions are unemployed. In this setting, it is the sole charge of the government to increase and maintain the good performance of health facilities especially in those areas hit by the conflict and other crises. Insofar, the provision of health facilities during crises tends to be cost-effective for school learners to access health services within the accessible school environment.

From the view of quality health services, the existing health facilities need to be managed by qualified medical personnel and practitioners to render quality health services to the affected communities. This, however, also involves the recruitment of qualified medical officers and certified health personnel with varied specializations of diseases. In doing so could help in reducing the outbreak of tropical diseases that are of the common incident in South Sudan. In addition, it needs the provision of enough medical equipment that would yield correct diagnoses of diseases and succeeding prescription of medications to the sick learners and parents. This may also enable asymptomatic patients to typically get all their medical prescriptions within the school neighborhoods for that matter. This essentially encourages the learners and school personnel to carefully avoid moving to remote places where they may fall victim to socio-economic insecurities and vulnerable child related trafficking and possible abduction.

Strategizing on Effective School Management and Transformational Leadership

The moral philosophy of each learning in common is to typically have an effective school management installed by the school governing body. The brilliant idea of having an effective school management correctly is to instantly realize quality education standard that can correctly answer the society needs. In addition, it calls for the system of education to solve the immediate problems of the wider community across different geographic and demographic boundaries. On some reasonable grounds, school management typically creates an enabling learning environment for children's wellbeing, hence, increasing literacy and numeracy components to occur efficaciously. In this respect, the school management refers to the successful operations of the school, the management of the human, material and financial inputs used in the facilitation of the learning process. In other operative words, school management is a dimensional process of leading the school towards socio-economic development through the optimum use of the human and material resources as well as fulfilling guided principles and concepts that help in achieving all the objectives of the school.

The importance of school management is geared toward shaping the teachers' development, determine the educational goals of the school, direct educational applications to achieve educational objectives, make recommendations on the regulatory practices of teachers' approach, find solutions for the problem between teachers and the classroom setting. The principal objective of school management centers on the practical functionality of learning. This is to accomplish the cognitive enhancement of both teaching and learning domains in a school environment through the effective binding of administrative apparatuses under the guidance of transformational leadership. However, there in common is a specific need of a local school leader to intentionally drive the social transformation and economic development of the school management. In fact, transformational school leadership is required during crises to effect swift changes of improvement in the school environment.

A transformational school leader ensures learners focus

entirely on their social studies by being considerate of marked individuality and charismatic in positively influencing and divinely inspiring them. Instead of using a specific set of problem-solving techniques, a local school leader involves students and teachers to come up with solutions to social problems as they naturally arise. This typically implies that effective school leaders focus on specific instruction, physical facilities and local people. By comparative advantage, local school leaders through their day-to-day actions, act in a professional and responsive manner and engage in regular self-reflection to realize rational learning outcomes.

Precisely, it is the social responsibility of the school management to look for resources of all forms and to ensure the obtainable possessions are well-managed. As an organizational commitment, the duty-bearers are typically head teachers, school directors, school administrative staff, responsible County Education Directors (CEDs), independent inspectors and supervisors, parent teacher associations, and the school based management committees. School management typically implies carefully running the school along the desired educational policies designed and adequately provided by a given country. This sufficiently takes into account all aspects of the school such as school rules and regulations, material and human resources, learning and teaching programmes, co-curricular activities, equipment, amongst others, and integrates them into a fruitful whole.

At the heart of its goal is that, education is the provision of a sequence of learning experiences to students in order to disseminate knowledge, values, attitudes, and skills with the ultimate aim of making them become productive members of society. This naturally brings us to a closer understanding of educational management as the process of planning, organizing, directing, and controlling the activities of an institution. This could be by utilizing human and material resources so as to effectively and efficiently accomplish functions of teaching, knowledge exchange, and research.

As a commitment to educating all learners, the National Policy of Education goes in pursuit of knowledge to bring about social, economic, and cultural development in society by focusing on human resource development through education. In this foreground, education, therefore, must typically have more relevant curricula and be dynamic so as to empower scholars to bring about desirable social changes. Meanwhile, it should be aimed at preserving the desirable aspects of our existing socio-economic and cultural tendencies. In this respect, the national developmental goals ordinarily require the professional management of education to bring about the effective and efficient functionality of educational institutions in the face of crises.

In obvious circumstances, emergencies stress school management in the short-term and long-term facets. At the micro level, classroom instruction is negatively affected. This could attribute to the issues to which the education policy makers ought to address through affirmative action plans. It is imperative that the role of an educational policy maker includes the monitoring of school size, class size, and private school choice. The policy makers should also assess school privatization and the positive values that schools are expected to transmit. On the other hand, at the macro level, the operational effectiveness of the comprehensive education system and administration drastically declines. This typically implies that the macro level should also take a closer look at teacher education and certification, teacher remunerations, teaching methods, curricular content, graduation requirements, and school infrastructure investment.

Indeed, predominant school management issues that may be exacerbated in possible emergencies may include increased need for hazard mapping and risk management. This is to identify schools and teachers under attack, level of damage of school facilities as well as those schools being used by armed groups. Likewise, school management places more considerable emphasis on schools being located in areas at high risk for natural and manmade disasters as well as in those communities which cannot access better and affordable educational opportunities. In addition, increased demand on the school to serve more and different student populations, especially the host school is converted to double shifts due to frequent incursion of refugees or displaced families. The degradation of community social systems during prolonged crisis may make the schools to be the last resource centers for life-saving messages, community gathering, or a safe space for all learners.

Further, some contributing factors may typically play unsolicited conditions, which do not yield anticipated goals of education. These may include the decreased parental involvement in education due to progressively increase in external pressures to meet the basic needs of their family as jobs, market demands, and transportation systems could be disrupted. Along this direct line, increased need for teacher support and management when teachers are knowingly exposed to the external predicament since the students can be negatively impacted by crisis. On this basis, teacher absenteeism and standard displacement voluntarily reduce the qualified teaching force as well as change in school resource management. Such activities require the community to take up school leadership and look for multiple aid organizations and education partners to provide confirmatory interventions.

To drive for success in the school environment, the head teacher should be surrounded by dynamic teaching force to properly appreciate an effective and efficient school administration. The position of the head teacher in any school at anywhere in the world is a demanding responsibility and difficult job. The head teacher is the accountable officer for the school and so is responsible for the effective management of human and material resources, the learning in the school as well as the safety of the learners and teachers. At the same time, the head teacher must typically work hand in hand with many key stakeholders to ensure that the school is supported morally and financially. Being an answerable officer means that he or she takes primary responsibility for many things such as the quality of education being delivered in his or her school, the quality and delivery of the school development plan.

In fact, head teacher is also responsible for the communications with local education managers like County education and Payam Offices for the purpose to coordinate all educational activities. In addition, the head teacher builds a strong school's complex relationship with the local community around so as to ensure the quality of the school governance. In light of this move, they are also responsible for the management of the staff to ensure that there is an effective communication with the staff and the School Management Committee (SMC).

Another key issue to carefully consider is an effective management of the learning institutions which may top the list of needs in the school situations. On conceptual certainties, school leadership has multiple roles to play during emergency situations in terms of direction and moral guidance. It is one of the key components to which education in emergencies could be advanced strategically and proportionally. In line of national goals of education, quality education is only achieved when the school leadership is purposefully focused on teacher professional development through career enhancements. From here, the main focus of the school organization is to raise the standard of education through modestly improving the academic success and social progress of the learners. However, this cannot be achieved without stage-managing on the effective school administration and planning to realize functioning learning activities.

Most importantly, educational planning is one of the areas

the school leadership should concentrate more especially on the basis when considering the current state of the affairs. This gives the head of the school and other members of the institution what they ought to do when the situation turns out to be so complex and volatile. After all, what is needed are progress and access to the learning activities that produce quality educational standards. Frankly speaking, effective school management remains the core area of emphasis to gently encourage inculcation of knowledge and skills for the teaching and non-teaching staff as well as the learners. However, given the quality of management in the school setting, the education system remains a hidden idea in the event that learning activities are brought on the knees during crises. For instance, during the COVID-19 Pandemic, in the context of South Sudan, all learning institutions were closed and none opted for online learning programs. This is because most of the education managers and actors were not so vibrant to devise an alternative commitment for learning to undoubtedly continue. Hence, the impact was so negative to some larger extent, especially on the school performance and the production of educational knowledge.

According to Ololube (2013), educational planning is concerned with the problems of how to make the best use of limited resources allocated to education in view of the priorities given to different stages of education for the need of the economy (as cited in Olambo, 1995 & Ololube, 2013). Apart from the operational planning of educational services during non-emergency situations, the planning for EIE is slightly different. As a direct result, it requires spontaneous decisions and actions designed to arrest unpredictable situations. To this point, educational planning during the crisis is an important tool to be adopted by school leadership to achieve learning outcomes within the school system.

As a result, such formal requirements should also develop a wider understanding of teachers with varied needs to be met.

In fact, good leaders take time to get to know their teachers, including knowledge of their families, interests, fundamental weaknesses, strengths, and development needs. In particular, it is important for the head of the school to know what motivates the staff, other team members and the entirety of the student body. It is imperative that human resource planning ought to be interconnected with the sustainable management of the day-to-day affairs of the school. It is also linked to the overall vision and mission of the school, since it is the collective effort of the human resources in and around the school to achieve the predetermined learning goals.

More recent studies have argued that appropriate course of action plans should include the contingencies for natural and human-made disasters, such as frequent earthquakes, tornadoes, floods, fires, chemical spills, and a host of other potential crises (Olambo, 1995 & Ololube, 2013). This calls for a holistic approach for the leadership of the schools to conduct emergency plans regarding the negative implications that might transpire within or outside the school settings. Indeed, planning during an emergency situation involves identifying levels of emergency and making significant decisions based on humanitarian and educational needs. The government, local community, and humanitarian actors can expend these necessities as strategic interventions for the success of the learning undertakings. In addition, it is also important to identify the category of the most marginalized people, disadvantaged members of the communities and visible minority groups. This can help the concerned administrative departments and line ministries to examine and determine the kind of basic needs required to support the affected communities at a particular time.

Universally, considering the school as the safe haven for learners, Cahill (2010) acknowledges that education offers safe spaces for learning, as well as, the ability to identify and provide support for affected individuals, particularly children and adolescents. As such, a plan, brought into the line is the provision of education during an emergency needs to give due attention and special consideration to issues that have to do with sustainability. In this case the projected activities only target educational operationalization countrywide. On the other hand, school planning is a major tool used by any implementing organization or individuals to predict events that may befall the nation or institutions at any time. The instructional structure of educational planning has been emphasized in the context of educational situations. Without meticulously planning for effective education prior to an emergency, then enlightening activities may typically bear great and unimaginable impacts.

Traditionally, given the degree of disasters and the considerable length of the emergency that has instantly stricken a given country, detailed operational planning is of paramount importance. In this respect, educational planning with preparedness in one's brilliant mind, carefully planning is habitually quick and mostly considered the responsive tool to adopt during crisis. Unlike management, school planning remains an element of local school leaders whose main aim is to organize moral support and peace-building activities using the valuable resources at their proper disposal. Smith (2009) has contended that schooling can provide safe learning and teaching spaces, psychosocial and emotional development of the peers as well as offering opportunities for learners to enthusiastically receive food and medical assistance. In this context, one would argue that schools may not possess the funds to conduct emotional and psychological activities, and this requires external supports from the NGOs, community members, and well-wishers.

In fundamental principle, careful planning during crises begins with the leadership at the top along with vertical leadership from the government down to school principals. This additionally includes the direct involvement of teachers, school nurses, and school officers to typically create safe schools. In the specific context of South Sudan, this crisis planning has not been given due attention as it has always been done by the administration of the United States and other forward-looking countries. Educational planning is an important aspect that needs to be taken into consideration before, during and after the gradual emergence of crisis and non-crisis situations.

Most importantly, some effective instructional methods in some school settings could be applied to encourage equal participation of all learners including girls who shy away from such negative instructions. For instance, HIV/Aids teaching messages may scare the girls, particularly when the way the content is delivered does not follow the conventional social and academic procedures. This entails a situation where an instructor perceives the female students as the only victims of the disease and all discussion centers on the girls. Based on the strategy of ECW, it could be gratefully acknowledged that applications of gender-sensitive instruction and the national curricula could reduce negative stereotypes which can undermine an equal learning environment for all. Consequently, this may lessen the discriminatory behaviors in the excellent school system, invariably leading to improve retention rate at the school level.

Nonetheless, what I am attempting to point out is that with or without educational resources, the school leadership can still organize radio talk shows on counseling activities. Such interactive radio talk shows may encourage the affected students, teachers, and other members of the school community so that they gain some resiliency and trust-building capacities. This is in line with the analysis of Smith (2009), which supports the idea of education to mitigate psychosocial implications and stabilizes the affected individuals to remain hopeful for their future. In this respect, imparting life-sustaining information and messages through radio programs to students and parents affected by conflict and other disaster-related causes play a crucial role during the crises.

Outstandingly, Cahill (2010) notes that education passes on critical lifesaving information on simple hygienic and potential health issues or the imminent dangers of explosive ordnance. In war-affected countries, school children often fall victim to landmines and other explosives planted by the adversary forces during war times. On the odd occasion, governments do not comply with their obligations to protect children and other vulnerable groups during emergency contexts. As such, it becomes the responsibility of everyone in the society including the well-wishers to offer practical skills on issues related to health, safety, preventive measures, and other precautionary issues. However, thanks to some donors who carry out a major role in ensuring landmines and other explosive ordnance in certain areas are identified and carefully removed for the safety of school children and the members of society.

Apart from lifesaving messages, education adequately provides a peaceful and democratic atmosphere that enables the children of the victims to forget the recent bad memories of what had happened or is happening during the crisis. As evidenced by Cahill (2010), children and people have the opportunity to escape an environment full of tragic memories and sad stories of what has happened to family and prominent community members. This implies that children do think on a daily basis of any sad reminiscences of what happened during the crisis. As a result, tragic memories sometimes expose children and youth to experience nightmares during sleep. It is important to bear in mind that specific approaches can be adopted at individual and community levels to focus on mental issues and moral development for children traumatized by conflicts such as mental illnesses. On the other hand, framing of psychosocial goals at the institutional level in groups to empower educational programs, is considered to be the best well-thought interventions.

At the human level of commitment and implementation of rights to education, education in an emergency considers the heartbreaking memories and sad stories of war to be often cleared off when educational opportunities are adequately provided. Such provision of educational activities was efficiently utilized in the aftermath of the Rwandan genocide. For instance, as children of Hutu and Tutsi were brought together under unified and coordinated teaching and learning activities so that they had to forget those miserable memories which happened during the genocidal war of Rwanda in 1994. If this could be adopted in South Sudan, it may support the survivors of war to recover rapidly from terrible incidents of wars and other naturally occurring phenomena. At some outstanding points, providing fully-funded scholarships to primary and secondary school teachers is principally an affirmative action worth-acknowledging and appreciating. Moreover, teachers from teachers' training institutes and vocational training centers, university staff of both public and private levels, should upgrade their professional standards so as to improve their teaching pedagogies and supervisory skills.

On a rare note, extant literature (Lisa, 2012) indicates that survivors experience difficulties with social functioning at work and school with friends, and also in their families. This is because they are traumatized and become pessimistic with life, including continuing with their educational journey. As noted by Dyregrov (2002), some individuals reportedly have withdrawn emotionally and socially and are unwilling to accept others and assistance (as cited in Lisa, 2012). Lisa (2012) underscores that psychosocial service providers need to be educated on how to deal with the survivors by focusing on intrapersonal and interpersonal losses. With the training of the service providers to deliver psychosocial support services, the affected communities or individuals would be assisted to gain resilience and preset hope during the crisis and the aftermath of the conflict-related events. Indeed, they would be able to cope with life normally despite ongoing crises.

As far as education in emergencies is concerned, due attention and resources need to be mobilized and given to school trainers to enable them to deal with affected and traumatized students, teachers and parents, particularly in the conflict-affected zones. To make a program an integrated one, the effectiveness of other economic health and nutrition interventions is directly related to that of provision of Water, Sanitation, and Hygiene (WASH) facilities in the schools. A lack of adequate and safe drinking water and WASH facilities coupled with poor hygiene, impacts negatively on the comfort of the school. Indeed, the possible contamination of food, lack of access to water, sanitation and hygiene services are also the leading causes of gastrointestinal illnesses and acute respiratory diseases among learners.

On square basis, learning space and good hygienic conditions may consider a safe water supply for drinking and washing hands and providing soap and maintaining regular hygiene of latrines. This also requires the school to maintain clean and tidy classrooms by limiting the presence of livestock from school compounds. It is the sole responsibility of each school management to ensure that stagnant water is drained out of the school ground and do away with litter and rubbish. In fact, malaria and respiratory related illnesses are the most leading killers of young children and the primary infections confronting adolescent children in all emergency situations.

To salvage the situation, safe drinking water as combined with good hygiene practices, can reduce gastrointestinal illnesses among learners. Nevertheless, when safe water and good sanitation facilities are provided, but there are poor hygiene practices, school gets fewer benefits of improved water and sanitation. On the other hand, WASH in schools provide general protection and also back up psychosocial and emotional wellbeing by bringing a sense of dignity and self-protection control for learners. However, to make these important contributions, waters, sanitation, and hygiene interventions ought to be carefully planned and executed in accordance with clear and strict standards. Typically, doing this requires high levels of technical support and guidance from the concerned specialists at every stage and programming cycles of Education in Emergencies. In some proportional advantages, those psychosocial support activities in the educational settings are geared towards sufficiently addressing the immediate needs of the affected individuals. These pressing needs should come from identifying the problems facing the victims, ranging from rape cases, attempted physical assault, and the disappearance of loved ones. Having identified the challenges, the service providers should keep in mind that the affected individuals gain resilience, hope for a better future, despite the ongoing crisis and its adversative consequences.

Undeniably, these survivors can be helped by psychosocial service providers through the provision of emotional and spiritual support, by advocating on behalf of the victims, or by offering necessary food and household supplies (Lisa, 2012). Though many writers did not talk of child soldiers as one of the critical areas that need education actors during crises to avail necessary interventions, it is essential education in emergencies should consider the disarmament, demobilization and reintegration of child soldiers into civil life. This is because, during armed conflicts, many youths join the armed forces voluntarily either to get food or feel secure in their neighborhood in case the conflict turns out to be a tribal war.

Local Community Involvement and Participation to Scale Up Education in the Face of Crises

Indeed, active participation of the school community in school affairs is typically required for the functional and vibrant system of education to flourish. The proper frames of reference are the direct continuation of holistic education during crises entail community involvement in all the decision-making processes of the given schools. On its abstract reality, a community is a group of people that occupies the same demographic and geographic area and share common characteristics of considerable interests such as political, social, economic, technological, and cultural aspects. To a larger extent, local community members are the backbone of the country's socio-economic development which keeps the system of education intact. Thus, the roles of the community in the context of supporting EiE should not be undervalued and underestimated. Therefore, when considering parental and community participation in education, it is important to think about it in terms of their role in allowing and promoting access to it education.

The term school community typically refers to the various individuals, groups, local businesses, and institutions invested in the welfare and vitality of a public school and its community including the neighborhoods and the municipalities which are served by the school. In this sense, schools are important communities for students and parents. During crises, educational outcomes, social and emotional competencies and critical thinking skills are all enhanced when learners have unhindered access to school environments where they feel safe and genuinely enjoy a sense of belonging and connectedness. This enables learners from diverse backgrounds to bring their personal thoughts, feelings, and possible experiences into the classroom. To me a school community is a congregation of the people intimately attached to a school, and these include teachers, school administrators, students, and the students' families.

Despite all odds of crisis, the determined school community actively cultivates respectful and supportive relationships among learners, teachers, and parents. Indeed, supportive relationships are the heart of the school community which ought to be supported by all means during emergency contexts. The interpersonal relationships create the school community ethos, the shared beliefs and values. The whole-school feeling exists to such a considerable extent that it drives the school as a community towards achieving goals. There is an idiosyncratic association between the school atmosphere created in schools and their learning environment. In this sense, strong communities are critical because they are often an important source of socio-economic connection and a moral sense of rightfully belonging. Indeed, voluntarily participating in a local community glued by positive attitudes, societal values and educational goals is an essential component to enjoying a fulfilling and sustainable life.

On abstract basis, EiE in many ways, is grounded on collective and collaborative efforts meant to scale up educational opportunities and activities in the face of crises. However, one would ask a question about the rather community members who may participate in the educational discourse during the crisis. The tentative answer to this fundamental question is that the community members are part and parcel of the different education and economic actors starting from the government, Civil Society Organizations, religious based-groups, private sectors, armies, and other organized forces. The unique combination of these stakeholders has vital roles to play in shaping the national education system both in emergency and non-emergency contexts.

On equal consideration, education stakeholders have been the backbone of the functionality of the learning during crises since the providers of resources that encourage the continuation of the schooling. From an educational viewpoint, it is imperative to say that collaborative determinations should be encouraged between the members of the community and the school leadership. At the national and local levels, combined efforts are essentially a leverage point that needs to be initiated and taken into consideration. In purely evolving terms, the reshaping of the national education system of South Sudan during crises should emphasize the practical applications of educational knowledge, skills and positive values from all works of life. Doing so may likely be a favorable accomplishment and giant step forward in protecting children and youth from different socio-economic predicaments and geo-political fatalities.

On the other hand, South Sudan Inter-Agency Network for Education in Emergencies (INEE) Standards feature community members to include a considerable variety of social groupings. The composition of community members includes village authorities, county commissioners, Payam and Boma administrators, PTA, religious leaders, mother and fathers, women and social advocacy group members, girls, boys and youth, people with disabilities, school administrators, among others. The well-thought representation and composition of stakeholders encourage positive participation for all, in a manner that leads to full achievement of national goals of education. In wider professional contexts, the composition of the school community could typically include the distinguished professionals, parents, stakeholders, partners, laymen, and women who reside in any given geographical setting. This tells us that all professional communities where the school is located should be mobilized fully to take part in the decision-making process regarding the plans of the school. This process should be aimed at creating a shared understanding of what would be the most critical areas of engagement and collaboration to keep the continuity of learning activities without interruption.

The support of parents and communities is essential to improving access to learning and succeeding realization of quality education in emergency and non-emergency contexts. If responsible parents do not feel the safety of their children in school or that the education being provided is not relevant, then their support for their children attending is likely to fade away. As a result of such negative impressions toward the schools, parents and communities may disengage themselves from an active involvement simply because they fear the risks, associated with the learning of their children and may oppose to the relevance of education. However, when community members are fully engaged in the affairs of the schools, they see it as a safe and protective environment which supports the welling and discovery of learning required by their children. On the same note, they realize the value of education to their children's prospects and stability of their community and society at large. It is thus, central to earnestly, consider the parental and community involvement and the barriers hindering their commitment so that the stream of EiE remains highly sourced and financially sustainable.

In addition, educational authorities and auxiliary actors need to consider each of these possible behaviors, and work towards reaching the highest level, where communities initiate and share all aspects of the decision-making process. Although parental and community participation can undoubtedly have a significant impact on access to and quality of education, the participation of the children themselves who are the target of the education being provided is equally important. One way to build effective community of learning is to involve children and latent students to be convinced of the safety, relevance and value of the education being offered. Indeed, if learners fear for their safety in school, they cannot be socially deemed to access to learn successfully. Addressing this requires ensuring meaningful and active participation from children at every stage of the programming cycle such as assessment, programme design, lesson delivery and extra-curricular activities and clubs. In addition, participation and accountability mechanisms are critical basis for realizing an effective learning outcome. It also means doing this from the very start of the programme, not once its trajectory is set to operate.

In the face of any crises, either being man-made or naturally occurring, the members of the community are affected directly or indirectly. In this sense, nature and the direction of their services could be jeopardized, consequently leading to the interruption of the education of their children. This points to the fact that education in its very nature is a collective responsibility advanced to help the needy populations during both emergency and non-emergency settings. Importantly, the participatory approach is geared toward meeting social and eco-friendly responsibilities to explore the defective mechanisms aimed at addressing multiple challenges.

To a larger extent, it is true that popularly consulted and well-mobilized community members have important contributions to make during crises. For instance, they can be involved through a participatory approach in the planning of the school activities especially in selecting the most appropriate response strategy and course of action. This does not mean that they should only be involved in the planning process, but also in the assessment and evaluation of the responsive programs to be implemented with due consideration given to gender sensitivity and social extensiveness. In this sense, much of the focus of educational activities during crises in the context of South Sudan should be lined up to discouraging discriminatory behaviors towards girls and women. Apparently, the apportionment of educational opportunities, counseling services, or other training prospects to be conducted either locally or globally tends to be the leading societal dynamics for involving and considering community members in the school settings.

Figuratively, Parents' Teacher Associations (PTAs), Board of Governance (BoG) and School Management Committees (SMCs) take the lead during crises since the social composition involves the community members and the government representatives tasked to monitor, supervise, and inspect the progress of educational activities in a given geographical area. This should focus on the sustainability of societal perspectives to consider educational programs that can realize behavioral change at the community and individual levels. Because of the inevitability to use education as a viable tool for intervening in any extraordinary circumstances, all community members are expected to participate fully and actively in a manner that reflects the needs of the affected communities. Such active involvement of community members practically translates into answering the national calls for tangible action during crises. As such, it is one of the obligations of every citizen to contribute to any slightly crisis that hampers the country's educational and economic progress.

According to the South Sudan Minimum Standards for Education in Emergencies (2012) "community members participate actively, transparently, and without discrimination in analysis, planning, design, implementation, monitoring and evaluating the education responses" (p. 8). From the outset of such social necessities, this calls for responding to the demanding educational issues that deserve any support of any form. In this sense, the community members are compelled to devise and adopt workable projections and implement educational activities in a more transparent and active manner. As a matter of fact, two things are particularly noteworthy, and that is the full and active participation of the members in the implementation and planning processes. In this respect, mobilizing the community members to participate fully and actively implies that education service delivery is a collective responsibility of every member of society. This means that all the community members should be consulted and mobilized, sensitized, and fully involved to participate in educational activities and opportunities for the improvement of the country's citizens.

By involving and mobilizing the community members in the decision-making process of the school, it energizes and reactivates their interests and energies to commit and implement educational activities based on the needs of the education system.

Hence, this suggests that community members are obliged to commit themselves to the implementation of educational programs and activities. As such, the roles of the community participants are multiple, and these typically include planning, designing educational programs, projects, and activities using the most participatory and collaborative approaches.

In a crisis situation where education is in dire need, local community members can still play a crucial role in improving the negative impacts through donations either in cash or in-kind, contributions of ideas and advice, offering manpower as well as other means. According to the South Sudan Minimum Standards for Education in Emergencies (INEE, 2012), members of the community are in an active and transparent manner that does not encourage discrimination of all forms in all areas including the planning of educational activities, analyzing, monitoring, evaluating and implementing educational activities and response. In fact, the community is integral part in undoubtedly helping the government and other well-wishers to design and implement educational programs in the letter and spirit. Apparently, every country that intends to improve the efficiency and effectiveness of its social, economic, and cultural domains in the face of crises, ought to consider the active involvement and participation of community members. This is because members of a community have resources and ideas, and they are willing and ready at any time to devote any kind of support once they are fully involved engaged in the process.

However, the roles that are supposed to be rendered to the country by members of the community are not so far realizable because of the fact that the government at times undervalues the position of the ordinary community members. Although the community members are not fully mobilized to be part of the education system, they should not fold their hands while contemplating the unfolding situation. This is because being ignored by the government could make them feel less genuinely concerned and they may opt not to take any responsibility in that respect. As such, in the absence of involvement of community members, there is a tendency that the roles are completely run by the government and its development partners. Hence, the anticipated learning results cannot be achieved in a tolerable routine needed by the population. Put differently, it could be admitted that the financial assistance that comes from the donor countries, ideally comprises donations from the ordinary communities of the respective donor countries. In this background, it is the role of the government and the school leadership to mobilize resources from the privileged and wealthy individuals so that they can provide any assistance of any form to the learning institutions.

In fact, the active non-participation of the community in educational affairs has widened the gap between members of different ethnic backgrounds with the wrong perception that education is the sole responsibility of the government. This has lessened the active cooperation and collaboration of the community towards improving the educational standards and has resulted in shaping some negative perceptions that have led to the spread of hate speech by the South Sudanese communities against one another. Given these reasons, the application of educational knowledge and skills to address the crises is the most effective tool to propel the country forward, economically, socially, and professionally. However, much as the members of the community desire knowledge and skills, learning has remained a necessity for all.

In my view, both the affected communities whether on the side of the rebels or the government must be mobilized, consulted, and fully involved in the decision-making process for quality education to be achieved. On this basis, educational programs and activities in the face of crises serve as a critical basis for defending children and minimizing the widespread high rate of illiteracy. By doing so will make them feel being part and parcel of the same system of governance of the national education system. Virtually, this confirms the reality that collective efforts geared towards learning can sufficiently realize the attainment of EIE across the country. Put differently, it will bring them together and form a common mindset to accept themselves as citizens who share common national identities and varied social beliefs. By the same token, investing heavily in education during any emergency context is more cost-effective in the context of improving the socio-economic domains.

On the other hand, charitable community-based forums should also be engaged to contribute to the wellbeing of the learners. In fact, some of the influential groups like Civil Society-based Organizations, religious based-groups, private sectors, armies, and other organized forces stand equal chances to play an integral part in the eradication of political and natural disasters. As far as education for girls is concerned, the community is expected to contribute funds and other material resources for the construction of single-sex boarding schools for girls. During crises, girls become victims, and if boarding schools are constructed, girls may under certain circumstances, be confined in the school premises.

In light of this, they may be fully engaged in their studies without going out to meet their fate. By doing so could significantly reduce the rampant early marriages and teenage pregnancies among the young girls of school-going age. Generally, girls become victims whenever they are day students because they may risk their lives on the way to and from the school. The tendency to harass schoolgirls during the crisis is a branded community concept where parents end up being accused of collaborating with culprits to marry them off, at their tender ages. As crises prolong, chances are high for girl spoilers to brainwash underage girls with petty things either cash or in-kind. Hence, they end up being impregnated or forced out of school by their parents to be married off instantly.

As time goes, with such unhealthy romantic relationships being entertained by male colleagues, the girls get lured into unprotected sex. As a result, they end up with unwanted pregnancies, forced-child marriage, and in the aftermath, they drop out of school. Nonetheless, to protect girls during emergencies, members of the community to which the girls come from should initiate and support brilliant ideas that confine them in boarding school premises. This may limit the activities of the girl spoilers since they may not intermingle socially with them and retain romantic relationships which sometimes lead to early pregnancies, hence, they drop out of school.

In one way or another, members of the community may contribute to meet the operational costs for the schools while the government pays the teachers. This is a fair deal that can encourage the continuity of learning during crises. Such efforts have been tried elsewhere during crises, and success stories were recorded. For instance, Sommers (2004) stresses that such coordination in Cambodia was considered straightforward in which the government addresses the salaries of teachers and expenses related to examinations while the member of the communities covered operational and running costs. This could be one of the most reliable means to keep the national education system intact as well as being capable of producing quality graduates needed for the labor market. This tells us that education is a shared responsibility and so each member of the civil society should provide a helping hand for that matter.

The Roles of the Humanitarian and Education Actors in the Face Crises

To a larger extent, the role of humanitarian workers and development agencies cannot be underestimated during crises. This is because partnerships of the humanitarian and education key players are crucially important to scale up educational services during an emergency context. Globally, the donor communities in light of mobilizing and delivering resources have been hailed for being key active players in the provision of humanitarian assistance as an important step forward. On charitable grounds, humanitarian organizations have been playing active roles in the provision of development and emergency support to the affected populations at the global level.

During emergency and non-emergency situations, donors deserve appreciation for their coordinated efforts to invest in education through a number of ways so as to build shattered lives of children who are in and out of school. Sommers (2004) asserts that humanitarian actors should coordinate their actions on the basis of three goals which include making communities less vulnerable, maintaining that their humanitarian service should not support the political and military agenda, and saving the lives of the affected population. Notably, their social support has been witnessed in wide-ranging backing in many areas of need such as technical support, supporting local communities in providing clean drinking water, proper hygiene and sanitation, food assistance, and other agricultural extension programs. However, their main focus has been largely on the humanitarian and relief assistance to the affected communities. Yet, the education sector typically receives low attention in practical terms of funding and technical management.

In a modern time of crisis, it is imperative that learners and school personnel have traditionally limited official capacities to access to clean and safe drinking water. Not only that, however, providing safe and hygienic sanitation facilities and information on basic health issues and related sanitization is an important part of physically protecting learners while in the school. This is basically important and should be raised up when potential health threats are even more widespread and families may be struggling to handle the state of affairs at home and also at the

Students of Master of Education in Emergencies posing for a picture in one of the workshops in Juba (Courtesy of 2017)

Students of Master of Education in Emergencies posing for a picture at the School of Education premises during the last paper. They were joined by the founder of GEWLP, Prof. Julia Aker Duany and arepresentative f rom Indiana University (Courtesy of 2017).

school setting. In South Sudan, it is invariably a known fact that the government has no financial capacity to properly provide fully-funded studentships to its local schoolchildren to take part in studies in different professional fields in other advanced countries around the globe. This is simply because of either lack of political will to do so or due to the economic meltdown that has plunged the country following the 2013 political crisis. As much as education is genuinely concerned, I typically emphasize that endowed scholarships are windows of greatest opportunities for students and teachers who are negatively affected by conflict and other natural disasters.

On a realistic basis, forms of donor support usually include monetary support through funding and technical provisions such as support, skilled labor, and knowledge exchange. Basically, the moral supports are aimed at instantly accessing education, supplying teaching and learning materials, and the provision of TLS. However, despite the lifelong commitments of the donor, I have carefully observed that the funding underscore for the construction of TLS can solely build a secure learning space. Based on my extensive experiences on the humanitarian grounds, the average budget allocated to construction of TLS in common is approximately 15,000 United States' dollars. On honesty ground, this can effectively be utilized to construct a permanent learning structure. On the other hand, the community can be mobilized to typically provide bricks and the said budget can be allocated to the necessary purchase of local building materials as well as paying the workers.

In addition, infrastructural construction spans from temporary to permanent ones. At some key points, they can go up to hardware constructions of schools and latrines as well as extensive renovation of learning facilities. However, according to Boyer, there are different somewhat scholarships that should be encouraged and honored by universities, including scholarships for discovery, integration, application, and teaching (as cited in

Darling and John, 2005). In doing so, the chief beneficiaries are able to rediscover themselves academically and professionally enlivened to be integrated into the professional community. This is in line with the sufficient knowledge and skills they may get, which are highly demanded by the labor markets.

On the other hand, such key provision of scholarships could also be appreciated if partially provided within South Sudan or elsewhere because something little at hand is better than nothing at all. According to Education Cluster South Sudan (2012), the South Sudan Minimum Standards for Education in Emergencies underscores that "coordination mechanisms for education support mean the structured group supports efforts to amply provide education for children and youth affected in emergencies through social activities like training, technical advice, resources, information at all levels, and resource mobilization" (p.11). In my own view, such teaching activities and training programs should be supported at any level of education and sector so that the principal beneficiaries naturally acquire quality skills and proficient knowledge for basic survival.

At the institutional level, scholarship opportunities are graciously overlooked and have little value in war-stricken countries. However, scholarships are very important in war-affected countries like South Sudan and other war-ravaged countries. This means that scholarships should be designed and willingly given to economically vulnerable students as well as those coming from low-income families. Substantially, this many create fertile grounds for students who really need to advance their educational careers in order to serve their local communities in various professional disciplines and intellectual capacities. For instance, the United States Agency for International Development (USAID) had previously offered master scholarship programs to train 35 South Sudanese scholars on secondary education and education in emergencies respectively. The first academic program sponsored and graduated 14 females from

Indiana University in an acknowledged master's program specializing in Secondary Education. However, the second program sponsored by USAID had 20 distinguished scholars, 12 women and 8 men. The mutual fund was implemented by Gender Equity and Women's Leadership Program (GEWLP) and was co-taught by distinguished professors from the University of Juba and Indiana University, respectively.

It is evident today that these young men and women who benefited tremendously from USAID–funded Master's programs are contributing positively to reshaping the education system of South Sudan in both public and private sectors. The author of this book is one of them who benefited from the USAID-funded Master of Education Project (MEP) that invariably led to a master of Education in Emergencies at the University of Juba. The ultimate aim of the program was to create a sustainable South Sudanese-led program, preparing the School of Education at the University of Juba to provide a Master in Education in Emergencies and to address the needs of educational institutions, teachers, and students affected by conflict. In fact, this is huge support which is worth and sincerely appreciating and acknowledging given at the appropriate time when a country is really in need of educationists.

Socio-economically, endowed scholarships are primarily avenues to financially-disadvantaged students in order to advance cautiously their educational and professional career pathways. A well-thought of scholarship merely provides some socio-economic opportunities for young people to merely earn an education that can positively impact on their sustainable lifestyles. Without support from an outside source during crises, learners may have trouble paying for the studies they need to enter the workforce and become positive contributors in their respective societies. Indeed, a generous grant allows students to typically focus on academic studies, increasing their chances of staying in school and graduating on time. For this reason, social changes of lifelong learners being recruited into the armed forces or falling victims are significantly reduced. It is imperative learners who receive scholarships have fewer financial concerns, have more time to study, and a greater chance of considerable success.

The social reality is that, some students may wish to continue with their studies, but because of limited learning or no learning opportunities, they may opt to drop out of school; on that account, leading to educational wastage at any level of education. So for one to satisfactorily accomplish professional aspiration under such charity adds weight to the continuous improvement of the country's education system. This typically entails raising the literacy and numeracy rates of the national education system in terms of educational standards. It is therefore, advisable that the government and the well-wishers should encourage and support scholarship opportunities to enable financially disadvantaged students and children from minority communities to pursue their professional skills and knowledge during crises.

According to the fundamental principles underlined in the INEE manual, it calls for donor agencies to fund government programs such as accelerating staffing, mobility, equipment, and technical support and training opportunities (Sommers, 2004). This respectfully suggests that humanitarian organizations and United Nations Agencies should consider funding educational activities just like the humanitarian assistance to which a huge financial budget is allocated, annually and solitarily. Irrefutably, it is a known fact that these agencies and other donors have so far invested much in education besides humanitarian activities in developing countries. The potential impacts of their adequate funding are physically noticeable in those countries including the Republic of South Sudan. However, many large-scale funding efforts are still needed and especially in the education sector.

Conversely, Hammond (2013) emphasizes the importance of education of children affected by conflict to be offered through the humanitarian and development assistance since education is one of the basic human rights. This would enable them to obtain necessary educational skills and life-saving information for basic survival and continuity of learning. In this specific context, humanitarian actors and domestic governments should responsibly exercise the universal humanitarian principles such as *Humanity, Impartiality, Neutrality, Independence, Voluntary Service, Unity and Universality*. In visible light of these fundamental principles, this may help the affected learning institutions to realize the shared values of human dignity, professional integrity and responsive solidarity.

On liberal grounds, these fundamental principles typically provide the charitable foundations for humanitarian action to implement donor funding in patient compliance to effective policies and specific requirements. Indeed, they are key to establishing and maintaining access to affected people, whether in an inevitable disaster or a complex emergency, such as armed conflict. Promoting and ensuring compliance with the fundamental principles in common are essential elements of effective humanitarian coordination. With mutual regard to essential humanity, human suffering must be addressed wherever it is invariably found. The purpose of charitable action is to protect life and health and ensure respect for human beings as well.

In light of neutrality, sympathetic actors must not take sides in hostilities or engage in controversies of a political, racial, religious and ideological surroundings. On the other hand, impartiality implies humanitarian action must be carried out on the basis of need alone, giving priority to the most urgent cases of distress and making no distinctions on the basis of nationality, race, gender, religious belief, class or political opinions. On independence ground, humanitarian action must be autonomous from the necessary political, economic, military or other objectives that any actor may hold with regard to areas where humanitarian action is being implemented.

Indeed, the principle of voluntary service represents the

social motivation uniting all those working within the humanitarian mission with a desire to support others. It is both a credible source of direct inspiration and an official statement of moral solidarity geared toward learning outcomes. This is directly preferred and acknowledged as part of the service expected by the broader school community. Likewise, the universality of suffering typically requires a universal response and specific educational programs. Universality is one of the humanitarian principles where key strengths are virtually present in every community affected by emergency. This principle also means diverse societies have a collective responsibility to support each other's development and to work together in partnership and solidarity during catastrophes, for the benefit of all.

In this sense, all members of the local community must be active in all key parts of the country so that even the hardest-to-reach communities can undoubtedly benefit from educational support when deserved. This does not mean the level of activities must always be the same nationwide. Without a doubt, the fundamental principle of judicial impartiality may amply justify that certain areas affected negatively need more support where the needs are greater. With regard to unity of purpose, school community and education actors must not discriminate when recruiting volunteer and constant teachers. They must ensure their active membership typically includes a broad spectrum of local people across the diverse ethnic populations so that humanitarian backing is reliably delivered to all people, by all people.

Predominantly, these fundamental humanitarian principles typically remain at the essential core of imperative necessity to help people in specific need during armed conflict, natural disasters and other emergencies. Moreover, protection services such as tracking unaccompanied minors, abducted and lost children should be collectively coordinated and be reunified with their parents or guardians. This can be successful through participatory coordination which may involve social workers, local community leaders, well-wishers, and even faith-based groups to carefully trace the movement and specific locations of these affected children. Noticeably, these children ought to be sent to school to acquire basic knowledge and social skills for economic survival in the foreseeable future.

In the familiar face of possible conflicts, besides other related emergency issues, it has been carefully observed that vocational and technical training opportunities have been so far ignored. Certainly, the focus has always been on formal education. It is worth stressing that, both informal and formal educational services have equal weight as they provide extensive knowledge and skills to the youths for basic survival in emergency and non-emergency situations. This calls for strategizing on funding programs that can unanimously support academic studies and vocational training activities.

Proportionally, key provision of vocational educational opportunities can offer practical skills and technical know-how to those who may not attend formal schooling. As such, the vocational training centers can reliably produce semi-skilled personnel needed by the country especially in areas of bricks laying, welding, carpentry making, just to mention a few. Setting up and funding vocational training centers so that the school dropouts could upgrade their skills would not only empower them to gain jobs but should also solve the problem of teenage pregnancy. The creative activities in these training centers may play active roles in absorbing school dropouts and training them in practicing small-scale businesses like agricultural extension activities, bread baking, tailoring, welding, just to mention a few.

It is in this extensive background that a recommendation is given to UN Agencies, International and National Organizations, Donor Communities, and education actors such as USAID, United Kingdom Agency for International Development (UKAID), Save the Children, United Nations

Jubilating Finalist Students at the University of Juba celebrating their last year academic Paper, Juba
(Courtesy of 2021)

Children' Fund (UNICEF), and United Nations Educational, Scientific and Cultural Organizations (UNESCO), among others that they should reconsider their funding towards education during the emergency and non-emergency situations. Remarkably, EiE is crucially important for investing in human resource development which can progressively reduce a widespread illiteracy and significantly improve the socio-economic development of the broader community. Indeed, such funding should be geared towards the professional development of human resources since the domestic government is not willing or incompetent to perform that noticeable activities. In this sense, I tend to believe that professional purposes and intellectual goals acquired through one's learning help a person to deal with difficult people and complex situations. It equips an individual with the management skills needed in the diversified global market. Focusing on professional motives in the education sector certainly remains an all-inclusive approach because it instills positive attitudes that can be used to build healthy relationships with others in the wider community.

On humanitarian grounds, EiE should focus on robust humanitarian partnerships and synergic efforts to quickly realize rapid, efficient, effective, and innovative education response. A critical scholarship offered through humanitarian assistance can merely make a big difference in one's lifetime through the acquisition of meaningful education. The money from a scholarship helps learners by allowing then to be more selective in how they scarcely spend their free time. Yet, such a scholarship should not be manipulative, corrupted, and abused by those in authority. However, the provision of such opportunities should be in line with the value of consistent peace with one vision of a fairer world and beautiful life. As far as professional capital in education is concerned, I believe that placing more emphasis on moral, spiritual, intellectual, and cognitive development in students during crises is crucially important. This may help learners to acquire applicable knowledge which in turn can be applied make the national system of education more relevant to answer the varied problems facing the country. In the process, EiE aims at promoting access, inclusion and equity for all learners.

On the other hand, both sections of the learning domains such as Arts and Sciences, are the central points of focus to develop knowledge and skills needed by notable individuals to compete in the expanded labor markets. Specifically, the training on Sciences, Technology, Engineering and Mathematics (STEM) should be reconsidered and advanced locally and proportionately at any level of education. Practically, STEM is a curriculum-based specialization in relation to the idea of educating students in four specific domains: Sciences, Technology, Engineering, and Mathematics. More importantly, these practical fields are comparable facets, which accentuate innovativeness and creativity for the young people to acquire knowledge and skills to harness the available natural resources for the benefit of the country. In advanced countries, for instance, these four disciplines help skilled personnel to play integral role in the sustained growth and stability of the national economy.

From the professional-based reality, STEM education creates creative and critical thinkers, which increases science literacy and numeracy. Noticeably, this enables the next set of generations to become innovators and role models in the advancement of better socio-economic growth and technological development. Because of ignorance of science education in South Sudan, no scientific innovators can work to establish and develop industries and factories, which are primarily tasked to produce consumable and usable goods and commodities. In this way, it is clear that most of the goods and services are virtually imported from the African region as well as from far afield oversea countries like Japan, China, UK, amongst others. On a humanitarian ground, many developed countries have invested heavily in the provision of humanitarian assistance to the vulnerable communities across the globe.

PART FIVE

Conceptualizing Teacher Professional Development in the Times of Crises

At the global spheres of social life, the teacher is the noble heart of education, and its paramount importance to the democratic society is strategically situated at the center of the academic curriculum. It is the role of a teacher to voluntarily give knowledge to people through education, and the local community intimately intertwines concerted efforts to mobilize valuable resources for that matter. In fact, extensive knowledge in teaching is the critical basis for advancing socio-economic measures which can be typically accomplished in human life.

Typically, it is in this background that they provide the power of education to today's youth, thereby giving them the possibility for ever better future. As a practical matter of fact, well trained instructors simplify the social complexity of learning and make abstract concepts accessible to all learners of different categories. In a more responsive atmosphere, teacher professional development increases teacher motivation, mutual confidence and life-long commitment to teaching. It gives a room for teachers to learn new skills and apply them in the classroom which can lead to a more thought-provoking and effective teaching environment.

In the first place, equipping the teaching force with rationalized information and contemporary pedagogical knowledge is worth-appreciating. The pedagogic skills offered to instructors through capacity-building programs could help in minimizing the fading learning situations during crises. According to Linda (2006), teacher qualifications tend to bear some connections on student academic performance and professional achievements especially in key areas of subject matter knowledge, instructional abilities, teaching experiences, and verbal communications. Through the lenses of teacher education, this basically depends upon fostering effective management and school leadership to plan and build the capacity of teachers. This could be done through organizing training programs and other ...regenerated intensive workshops to equip institutional administrators and teachers with effective leadership and administrative skills.

Certainly, effective school management continues to be the core area of emphasis to encourage instilling of knowledge and skills for the teaching, non-teaching staff and the learners. In the course of sufficiently advancing teacher professional development programs, school administrators constitute the essence for providing the professional growth, that is, both relevant and effective in the socio-economic makeover of the education sector. The institutional commitment should focus on creating, implementing, and sustaining professional learning opportunities that are meaningful to teachers. Definitely, such efforts can increase student learning outcomes, hence improving the wider education system.

Given the fact that education can take place almost anywhere, a safe, accessible and comfortable learning space remains the priority. This creates confidence in learners to attend to school in massive number and momentously improves the ability of the teacher to conduct structured learning activities and for students to expressively participate in the learning accomplishments. In an emergency milieu, some learning centers and educational spaces may not be safe, secure, and accessible for a number of reasons.

Undeniably, TPD should be designed in order to be contextually relevant to the needs of the communities. Thus, TPD should entice effective learning and teaching activities especially in a crisis where quality education is significantly compromised. This requires strategic planning discourse to be adopted to streamline the teacher professional development programmes in the schools. As a matter of fact, one of these roles of an institutional governance is to scale up effective TPD planning in the ordinary affairs of the school setting. This strategic planning could be carefully adjusted according to situations in order for the schools to run effectively and efficiently. In an academic atmosphere, educational planning figuratively signifies an effective alternative to effectively manage educational activities.

Obviously and relatively, the teaching profession remains the lowest valued occupation in South Sudan and perhaps in other parts of the world due to low remunerations. However, it could be worsened by any humanitarian catastrophes since the national resources may be diverted to defense and national security sectors in case of a man-made disaster such as armed conflict. In an effort to help schools remain active and serviceable to communities, teacher training is one of the best means that helps education to achieve its intended aims during an emergency situation. With this in mind, Cahill (2010) recommends that, in emergencies, it becomes necessary to prepare them to better detect emotional and learning problems in order to treat the affected children and have them re-engaged in a conducive learning environment. In an emergency context, trained teachers play vital roles in identifying students and parents with traumatic conditions and devise better means and mechanisms to address the incidental implications of trauma.

As much as the training of teachers is genuinely concerned, emphasis is placed on the dynamics of learning and instructions. This means that the learner-centered approach and teacher-centered strategies are mixed so that learning becomes cooperative and participatory to arouse curiosity among the learners. The bottom line of this teacher training reality is to direct the teaching and learning activities to be focused on the physical, psychosocial, and cognitive needs of the learners. From the perspective of the teaching profession, they are believed to be

Some of the Teachers from Peace Secondary School in Juba, posing for a group photo at the school premises
(Courtesy of 2021)

Some of the exciting Law Students of the School of Law, University of Juba showcasing their professional dressing codes as potential lawyers a few days to their final year academic paper
(Courtesy of 2021)

active agents of institutional support and social change during an emergency and non-emergency situations. This is because teachers have multiple roles to play such as briefly noticing the hostile environment and then confining the students to the school environment when a spontaneous fight happens.

Moreover, they help to identify children with trauma and then devise means of helping them to cope with the prevailing traumatic situations. Even more, trained teachers are resourceful persons in the established community who provide quality education during an emergency crisis. Training of teachers is a critical component of any policy which aims at properly maintaining high standards of teaching in the universities and colleges (Prem, 2005). With the knowledge base acquired, education remains a potential tool to be used in the long run to solve the needs of society, especially for post-reconstruction societies.

In capitalizing on effective TPD programming, it is imperative that such TPD should include the top three types of teacher professional development which are periodic workshops, in-class observation, and single-session training, and should be content-rich. In unanimously adopting a lively teacher education, these are aligned with three theories of teaching such as child-centered, teacher-centered, and mixed teaching methodologies. Each element can be substantially improved by keeping a few general principles in mind while leading professionalism in the teaching profession. In the same note, TPD is a crucial component of the national education system that leads to quality instruction.

In simple description, teacher professional growth is any type of continuing education effort for them to upgrade their teaching skills and knowledge of the subject content. It allows them to improve their teaching skills and competent knowledge, which in turn boosts the learning outcomes of learners. In the context of quality education, teacher professional development implies the continued access to training, continuous professional development, and support on teacher's extensive knowledge of subjects and their abilities to use the most effective teaching methods. It is an essential component of teacher training that ensures the effective delivery of quality education at all appropriate levels of learning.

Alternatively, teacher professional development typically includes both active pre-service and in-service training programs. In its basic understanding, pre-service training refers to the organized teacher training programs received by teachers before voluntarily entering a classroom and beginning to teach. In consequence, recruitment of new teachers who have no teaching backgrounds may need well-organized pre-service training procedures. For instance, all the graduates of the school, colleges, and institutes of education, both in public and private institutions of tertiary learning, should be subjected to pre-service training programs and afterwards certified as professional teachers before they join the teaching job.

On the direct contrary, in-service instruction refers to the continued training opportunities given to teachers after they have begun teaching in classrooms. This training is offered to the already practicing teachers to improve their knowledge base in subject content and teaching skills. It is difficult to plan and execute creative opportunities for teachers to continue to build their skills if professional training opportunities are not capitalized for teachers. Professional development for teachers takes place at different levels such as in county education centers, schools, or even on a classroom or individual basis. On most rare occasions, learning can take place in formal or informal settings. This alone provides a sense of professionalism and responsibility for teachers while performing their professional duties.

In a similar fashion, it is noted that the most effective professional development programs engage a vibrant team of teachers to focus on the needs of their students. Considerably as collaboration in the learning context is concerned, they learn and solve jobs related problems together to ensure students achieve academic and professional success. Indeed, appropriate development can help new and experienced teachers develop the skills they need to feel confident in the classroom while delivering the content to learners. For knowledge sustainability, experienced teachers should spend their whole careers developing new skills in response to the challenges they encounter in the course of fulfilling their teaching profession. However, new teachers have not had a chance to build their own professional resources. Without a doubt, effective professional development helps teachers to shape career-long learning and promotes some growth of mindsets of teachers and learners alike. It is widely agreed that an effective professional development program helps teachers to shape career-long learning skills; hence keeping them abreast with the current development in the teaching profession. In simple connotations, TPD programs that are well planned and with specific content directed through pre-service and in-service training facets may boost learning outcomes and promote a sharp mindset of learners.

The ultimate aim of TPD is to make great teachers who can deliver good teaching and learning activities. It is apparent that excellent teachers are better placed to teach students and make them learn effectively. However, good teaching is a result of teachers having access to continuous learning opportunities and professional development resources to better equip themselves. To become good teachers, it is imperative the needs of learners are met to enable them to perform above grade level. Teacher professional development encourages teachers to be active participants in their own learning and ensures that students and teachers alike are eager to learn. When you provide learning and support for your teachers, you communicate that the school community values the work they perform and desire them to grow professionally.

Regarding the setting of teacher professional development, formal settings may properly include conferences, professional courses, seminars, retreats, and workshops. While in an informal setting, such opportunities for teacher professional development may include independent research or investigation, peer learning initiatives, or even just chatting with a colleague in the staff room. During emergencies, teacher's necessary qualifications and professional backgrounds matter a lot since it equips teachers with new knowledge and skills which revolve around effective delivery of content and management of the learning process. Without a doubt, effective instructions are designed to meet the varying needs of all lifelong learners participating in the schooling. Nonetheless, a design of teachers' training programs should not discriminate against children with disabilities, children from visible minority groups, and economically disadvantaged learners.

It should be mentioned that students with different learning abilities ought to be actively engaged in the learning process in order to understand the relevance of learning content and be protected in their learning environment. It is imperative teachers feel confident and competent in their professional role as well as with the content of the curriculum. The basic content to train teachers may include literacy, numeracy, core subjects, and critical life skills. However, training teachers to be only competent in the basic content is not enough. Teachers need to be intentionally introduced to both learner-centered and mixed teaching approaches to meet learners' expectations. In the context of South Sudan, increasing teachers' professional capacity is of reasonable interest to the government. Though NGOs are putting some efforts to train teachers for short courses, however, lack of professional development resources for teachers can be discouraging. In times of crisis, designing and implementing teacher development, programs should center on the actual and evolving needs of both teachers and learners.

Most importantly, there should be a clear link between the standard curriculum, rights to education, learners' needs and expectations of the parents, and the training of teachers. In South Sudan, teachers' education levels are low and working conditions are unfavorable. These combined challenges facing teachers have negatively contributed to the lack of lasting changes in classrooms such as the application of ground-breaking learning materials and streamlined teaching approaches. Sincere speaking, teacher well-being remains a primary element of teacher professional development efforts. This alone can ensure the effective delivery of content in all learning and teaching situations. As crises intensify, the essential quality of teachers and teaching remains crucial not only in the local school system but also in the academic performance of the learners.

In this essence, the recruitment of qualified teachers and adequate motivation is moderately imperative. It is significantly important for the subject content and teaching methodologies to train teachers to reflect the requirements of learners and prepares teachers to respond to changing needs in an emergency context. Teachers and other education personnel should receive periodic, relevant, and structured training skills as aligned to the needs and circumstances of the school term. While professional development is often disrupted during disasters and armed conflicts, education in emergencies can open up windows of opportunities to provide supplementary training and support to teachers proactively working in affected communities. It is important to recognize that teachers have limitations and are affected by emergencies. Thus, teachers ought to be given their own psychosocial support structures equipped with the skills needed to extend similar psychosocial support services to learners.

Furthermore, naturally depending on the nature of the crisis, feasible capacity-building programs such as inclusive education approaches, gender sensitivity, disaster risk reduction (DRR), conflict mitigation or conflict resolution skills, peace building education are significantly relevant. In an ideal world, inclusive education refers to a process of addressing and responding to the diversity of needs of all learners through increasing participation in learning, cultures and communities, and reducing exclusion from education and from within education.

In an educational reality, an inclusive education aims to mainstream students with special needs in a flexible learning environment for acquiring standard education that optimizes their potential for holistic development. Entirely, it provides a better quality education for all children and is instrumental in changing discriminatory and cultural attitudes toward children with disabilities. In this way, schools should provide the non-discriminatory context for a child's key relationship with the world outside their families, enabling the development of social relationships and academic interactions.

On tolerant grounds, inclusive education implies that all children of the school going-age have the right to quality education and lifelong learning. According to Hayes, Turnbull, and Moran (2018), most students with disabilities in low-end and middle-income countries are either not receiving a quality education or are denied access to education altogether. At the school setting, teachers should be trained, buildings should be renovated and learners should receive manageable learning materials. Likewise, at community level, humiliation and discrimination must be undertaken and community members need to be educated on the benefit of inclusive education.

From the educational perspective, the requirement for inclusive schools is to educate all children together. This means that the schools have to develop ways of teaching learners which mutually respond to sole academic differences and professional needs so as to benefit all the children. In practical terms of a social aspect, inclusive schools should typically change social attitudes towards those who are in some way different by educating children together. This will help in creating a just society without discrimination of all sorts. This means all children in the similar classrooms and schools have equal access to learning opportunities without discrimination on the basis of gender, race, ability, disability, and favoritism.

By taking into account the inclusive education, this implies that inclusive education embraces the philosophy of universally accepting all children regardless of race, size, shape, color, ability or disability with support from school staff, students, parents and the community. Indeed, special education and general education teachers often work together to develop a standard curriculum and create a positive student culture. This means all children in the similar disabilities, or schools have equal access to learning opportunities without discrimination on the basis of gender, race, ability, disability and favoritism. The benefits of inclusive education increase social, motor and interpersonal skills. This means that all learners regardless of race, learning abilities, ensure that education policies, practices, and modern facilities respond to the diversity of all students in all socio-economic and geopolitical contexts.

In a reality check of inclusive education, there are recognized four social dimensions of inclusive education such as mutual exclusion, segregation, inclusion and integration. During crises, exclusion occurs when students are directly or indirectly prevented from or denied access to education in any form. Likewise, segregation proceeds when the education of students with intellectual disabilities is provided in separate environments designed or used to respond to particular or various impairments, in isolation from students without disabilities. Yet, social integration is a process of carefully placing familiar persons with disabilities in existing mainstream educational institutions, as long as the former can adjust to the standardized necessities of such social and democratic institutions.

As an ultimate point, inclusion involves a process of systemic reform embodying changes and modifications in content, teaching methods, approaches, structures and strategies in education to overcome barriers. The vision is equally serve and to provide all students of the relevant age range with an right and participatory learning experience and environment that best corresponds to their specifications and preferences. In this modern sense, promoting inclusive education is important to understand what inclusive education means, and to recognize the diverse settings for students with disabilities that are typically encountered around the world (Hayes, el al. 2018).

To benefit all learners, inclusive education should be prioritized in which all children with different learning abilities learn together with others. The concerted efforts of EiE can change the system to accommodate everyone especially in areas of problem-solving, support, and successful collaboration to overcome barriers to active learning and participatory participation. However, moral inclusive education is an approach that looks into how to transform the education system in order to remove barriers that prevent children with disabilities from participating fully in education. In most cases, the formidable obstacles may be linked to profound disability, ethnicity, gender, social status, poverty group, and socio-economic backgrounds. To a larger extent, provision of inclusive education looks at three areas such as educational, social, and economic aspects.

From the across-the-board education perspective; inclusive education should also consider the economic status of learners. This implies that establishing and maintaining schools without discrimination on the basis of disability encourages children from different backgrounds to learn and cooperate together. This is likely to be less costly than setting up a complex system of different types of schools specializing in different groups of children. Besides, understanding key inter-sectoral linkages may be necessary such as the provision of health and proper nutrition, water, hygiene and sanitation, and child protection to pave the way for quality education to prevail.

In this respect, cementing strong benevolent synergies and collaboration with other agencies and organizations are encouraged to provide a rapid training program in specific subject contents and assessment of learners. As these training programs may not effusively provide the support deserved by all teachers, it may become necessary to identify teaching gaps and plans to meet those training needs. In all cases, during the teacher learning cycle exercises, educators receive the best support from their professional colleagues and well-wishers in the wider community. This is constructively important when comparative thoughts and collaborative efforts are virtually explored extensively, and pedagogic approaches are straightaway employed.

Prime Essentials on Programming Teacher Professional Development

As far as teacher professional development is contextually relevant, the teaching force is properly equipped to support deep learning and teaching activities through ongoing learning. Indeed, intellectual mastery of one's teaching subjects is the sole responsibility of an education system to train teachers to be masters of their own professional destiny. Effective teachers should typically focus on improving certain areas where apparent weaknesses in teaching pedagogies are noted approvingly. For rare instance, deep learning should be focused on key subjects like Physics, Biology, Mathematics, Social Studies, Christian Religious Education and Geography.

Indeed, mastery of subject content is an important milestone for painstakingly building the capacity of teachers during and after crises of all sorts. Providing robust TPD programming activities that support specific instructional strategies and coaching abilities in specific subject areas implies an improved delivery of subject matter to the learners. For instance, a practice of effective use of arithmetical calculations in organized learning sessions may help science teachers to understand student metacognition based on a teacher's structured lessons.

More importantly, teachers play an important role in the lives of learners in terms of personal, moral, and social development. They can positively influence learners' behavioral change in terms of positive attitudes, which can help learners to solve their problems, develop cognitive, social and emotional skills. Prospective teachers realistically achieve this by constructively engaging learners through fun and interactive activities in the course of teaching and learning spheres. In an educational reality, training of teachers is one of the most important tasks, especially in emergency context which should be embraced unconditionally.

In emergency situations, both certified, instantly recognized teachers, and uncertified teachers have to address the needs of children affected by crisis. Their training needs are different in notable addition to teaching pedagogies, they also require trainings on coping and responsive mechanisms. TPD typically comprises of training on pedagogical knowledge, content-specific pedagogy and effective classroom management. This informative understanding of learning focuses on the subject specialized teaching approaches to carefully teach children to read, do mathematics, science, and other pedagogical roles. Indeed, student assessment and social engagement are supported with the key provision of teaching aid and learning materials for effective learning outcomes. There are various training models to be adopted for a face to face training such as collaborative professional development, which can be specifically designed on one-to-one coaching activities.

The recommendation is to structure the teacher training on

the accepted model aligned to the national teacher competency framework. This should contain well-defined hours of training, targeted audience, and contact frequencies. Nevertheless, it does not matter whether being refresher pieces of training, teacher learning groups, or supplementary pieces of training. In the key component of TPD, the overriding activities for effective teacher training include core and mandatory training programs which have professional recognition and learning relevance to longtime trainers. These span from training teachers on basic teaching pedagogies and understanding the emergency context to serve the needs of divers learners. It is often a unique challenge to positively identify and recruit qualified teachers to take on effective teaching and learning spheres of considerable success. However, some non-profit organizations which are implementing EiE tend to depend on the minimum qualification criteria set forth by the national Ministry of Education without indulging to add some needs-based pieces of training in given geographic contexts. In such rare cases, the necessary majority of the teaching staff do not possess the prior teaching and classroom management experiences.

Under these core professional packages, training on educational roles, content-specific pedagogy, psychosocial support activities and effective learning management could be typically offered. Nonetheless, effective implementation of core and mandatory training activities could be conveniently divided into some generated modules respectively. First, cultural orientation and elective induction to traditionally teaching have been hailed to be one of the needs and effective means of properly training teachers to honorably discharge their intellectual activities adequately. This is because basic teaching pedagogies, lesson planning and scheming, learning objectives, and practical use of teaching materials have been emphasized based on the experiences. In key addition, contextualizing local and low-cost materials, effective classroom management, child development, and learning needs top the list of effective TPD management. Likewise, content-specific pedagogy is another possible avenue for managing teacher education effectively during crises. In this respect, teaching literacy skills and the paramount importance of carefully teaching official language of instruction in early grades is another alternative to keep the teaching force proactively enliven. This gently encourages the application of basics teaching fundamental language skills such as the use of visual and kinesthetic styles of learning to learn mathematics, basic science, and concepts of life skills at upper primary level.

As far as effective TPD is concerned, adopting blended professional development requires some greater insights and approaches of training teachers. In this sense, supplementary training is the purpose of EiE to ensure that teaching personnel has the relevant knowledge to address the needs of children who have undergone trauma due to conflict. Supplementary training should primarily focus on orientation about life-saving messages, child rights and protection, psychosocial support, peace education, specific gender and conflict mitigation. In addition, training teachers on positive discipline is also essential to enthusiastically promote positive and respectful interactions in and around the school environment. This should form part of a comprehensive pre-service and in-service teacher professional development programme for supported teachers.

Then again, positive discipline can be a difficult subject in contexts where corporal punishment and other gender-based violence are widespread and not seen as an issue. Given the context of emergency, training teachers on positive discipline should be used even more widely when they are exposed to serious stress and insecurity as a result of different dynamic factors. In many contexts, local community members encourage the use of corporal punishment in the school as the best methods to discipline learners to ensure good behavioral change and success of learners can be attained. As with all teacher development initiatives, training on these TPD themes should be followed up with the regular on the job coaching and mentorship.

Moreover, teacher learning groups and circles are aimed at gathering teachers who come together to share their work, successes and challenges in order to help one another. Teacher learning groups and circles are a form of professional development where teachers reflect upon and learn about teaching in their own context and as base on their own classroom experiences. In fact, such training programs typically offer a space for teachers to work together in order to find creative solutions to their challenges, therefore they are positioned to provide each other with valuable support. Primarily, the goal of such professional platforms is to reinforce teaching concepts that were adequately explained, explored, experienced, and enacted during training, and to support teachers' well-being in the face of challenging job obstacles.

On the hands-on approach to get more rapidly solution to learning events during emergency situations, teacher learning groups could be typically structured like guidelines with already defined professional topics. These could be semi-structured such as refresher training could be need-based as identified through school monitoring, classroom observation school visits. The topics covered through refresher training could be themes under core training and should meet the sole aims of supplementary training. Furthermore, refresher courses offer an excellent opportunity to teachers to reinforce their concepts or to introduce changes to the existing learning materials.

In fact, need-based instructions should be customized and accurately determined by different education stakeholders to ideally move the course of actions for an active learning to be realized in every academic cycle. In this respect, focusing on the subject content and incorporating active learning approaches in the classroom settings tends out to be the best means of developing teachers. In an effective education system, training teachers to learn and apply new knowledge and skills to improve their teaching performance in the course of discharging their professional duties is the desired learning upshot. A two-way teaching practice makes great sense in the teaching profession. In this respect, collaboration in the training of teachers is an important aspect which school leaders and the wider school governance bodies should capitalize on, for the interest of the national education system.

TPD programs that help educators develop peer observation strategies, data streaming communication protocols, co-teaching models, and more teaching characteristics are vital bases for advancing quality teaching and learning in the face of crises. Supporting teacher collaboration through active learning efforts and a continuous cycle of training may improve the teaching pedagogies on each content area. Adequately providing a collaborative learning space for teachers to share their ideas collaboratively in the context of the learning domain is one of the key aspects of developing the capacities of teachers.

For obvious reasons, to raise student achievement in practical terms of student academic performance requires teacher collaborative efforts and best TPD programming. This should be through forming a vibrant learning team to share different aspects in terms of content and real-life circumstances to improve their teaching pedagogies. Since properly understanding of child protection and academic minors' civil rights mutually reinforces the concept and practices of EiE, it is equally important that all stakeholders have a common understanding of this commitment. Applying the principles of child protection and child rights in schools and learning environment is also easier and more effective if the parents, the community and children share their mutual understanding and obligations. It also has the potential to improve relationships at the household level between parents and children, on one hand. On the other hand, it improves the complex relationship and professional synergies between the teachers and the wider school system.

Consequently, training teachers on this important theme should be coordinated with providers of the training outside of the school. In light of this practice, parents can and should be reached with this important component through the PTAs, SMCs and Board of Directors or Board of Governors. One useful resource for doing this is the child protection sessions for parents and caregivers as an integrated program. Although the training of teachers on these topics should be provided immediately as part of induction, the actions for children, parents and community needs to be programmed sympathetically, especially in all emergencies.

An active learning and teaching activities imply effective learning outcomes. This is already demonstrated in the theory of andragogy which tells us that adults have a need to direct themselves, use prior experience, solve real-world problems and immediately apply new learning to current teaching responsibilities. In simple terms, learners have an inborn need for opportunities to develop learning autonomy, mastery of content, and purpose in their work. This is true and an important role a teacher should deliver in the face of crises. However, this does not come out of the blue, but through training teachers to improve their instructional capacities and abilities to deliver the content effectively and efficiently.

On the other hand, instructional coaching is a non-evaluative way to create opportunities for ongoing observation and giving feedback. In other kind words, it typically provides a reflection and improves teaching and learning practice for both learners and teachers in the given subject content. This is true in the sense that to fast-track areas of pedagogic weaknesses where there is an existing knowledge gap to be filled by experienced colleagues or external consultants. This is to ensure the quality deliverables with the perspective of the teaching profession are practically attained. It is also imperative to provide teachers with the substantive, specific and timely - feedback to enable them to reflect and act upon those frames of teaching feedbacks. Practically, this is one of the best learning and teaching practices for instructional abilities and content improvement which should be encouraged during the emergency and non-emergency contexts. Practically, this may include the framework and written documents used in classroom instruction, like textbooks, teaching and learning aids, and the syllabi that help teachers plan classroom activities.

In formal education systems, the syllabus is usually developed at the national level while non-formal education curriculum may be developed by other groups and in line with an extensive consultation with the local government. Regardless of the considerable number of materials available, teachers are reasonably expected to eagerly follow a set framework and ensure students achieve certain levels of learning objectives. While they may have little control over the curriculum, it may be possible for teachers to incorporate important life skills and peace education messages and content during modern times of emergencies, post-reconstruction periods and early recovery. These new messages and content may help save a student's life or amply provide protection, expand learner knowledge and understanding of the world, and how they can lead productive and peaceful lives. These life skills help learners to develop skills needed to find local employment opportunities based on one's specific areas of specialization. Noticeably, qualified teachers, together with their direct supervisors and the creative community, may be able to enthusiastically promote important messages using innovative teaching approaches such as student-centered and mixed pedagogical approaches.

PART SIX

Measurement and Assessment of the Learning Endeavors

Measurement and independent evaluation are the direct opposite of the same coin of standard checks of quality education. In most cases, they should go hand in hand with the continuous improvement of learning possible outcomes. Both remain an important constituent that deals with the comparative study of learners' intellectual abilities, learning outcomes, aptitudes, academic and professional interests, their personality, moral values, and varied attitudes. Specifically, precise measurement and evaluation help teachers to assess teaching and learning activities so as to arrive at some convenient results. However, standard measurement and evaluation can be used objectively and scientifically to carefully compare, correctly classify, naturally select, and find out true measures about the considerable progress of learning and teaching activities.

On a value-point scale, measurement is typically used for one sound basis for classification and comparison of learning needs and to adopt appropriate educative measures as well as avoiding possible failures and frustrations. All these naturally require the application of meaningful measurement and evaluation of learning activities. According to Sidhu (2005), *"measurement serves as a tool in increasing the effectiveness, efficiency, and output of the school (p. 21)*. From the academic context, measurement implies an action of measuring something to determine the quantity and the value. In linking it to instruction, educational measurement implies the use of school valuation and the analysis of data obtained from learning assessment to properly understand the abilities and proficiencies of learners. As far as quality learning is concerned, assessing the learning end result involves measuring the progress of schooling against identified learning objectives as aligned to national educational aims. It also fosters reliable learning outcomes and enthusiastically promotes social responsibility amongst teachers, education authorities, since it is a vital tool in fostering quality educational outcomes. Within the context of assessment and monitoring, evaluation and judgment are interchangeably applied.

It is worth-mentioning that both elements of monitoring and evaluation are simultaneous tools applied to the content. In its simple meaning, monitoring is about checking progress against plans. At some points, it is termed as terminal evaluation to mean summative. This assesses the progress made towards the outstanding achievement of the pre-determined objectives in the end of training program to provide a critical basis for decisions on the future course of action. Its consistent findings and specific recommendations are frequently used to decide whether or not to satisfactorily adjust the specific instructions or when a new phase of teaching approach is under practical consideration.

On the foreground, evaluation plays diverse roles in the life of a student. However, some of which they may be more aware of the specific focus of assessment than others. It is widely accepted that students' learning patterns, educational focus, and efficient allocation of time will be directly influenced by well-thought out judgments. In meaningful learning situations, educational assessment represents the creative process of meticulously documenting, usually in measurable terms, knowledge, skills, attitudes and beliefs. The overarching goal of assessment is to focus on the individual learner, the needs of the learning community, the social institutions, and the education system as a whole.

At its best, assessment has many functions such as capturing student time and attention, generating appropriate student learning activity, and providing timely feedback to which students should pay much attention during their studies. In key addition, assessment helps students to internalize the discipline's standards and notions of equality as well as generating marks or grades which distinguish between students who pass or fail their prescribed studies. To evaluate something is to appraise and rank its quality, a fierce determination of its moral worth and value. Comprehensive evaluation is typically meant independent appraisal or assessment with respect to some set standards. Evaluation is a process wherein the parts, processes, or results of a program are examined to see whether they are satisfactory relative to the learning outcomes and goals. In fact, evaluation in education is a process by which we form a judgment about the value of the educational status or achievement of them. Assessment plays a major role in how students learn, and the teacher teach besides lifelong learners' motivation to learn.

Functional assessment is used for various purposes such as evaluation for learning in which it helps teachers gain insight into what students understand to plan and guide instruction and provide helpful feedback to them. Likewise, assessment as learning helps students to develop an awareness of how they learn and use that awareness to adjust and advance their knowledge so as to take increased responsibility for their learning. Equally important, emphasizing appropriate methods of assessment on the basis of formative and summative aspects of learning is a sure means to ascertain the learning outcomes on the content given to the learners. This can enable the teaching conclusions to be evaluated and documented so that strategic planning with regard to improving learning is literally devised and in the end implemented. In fact, learning outcomes in form of extensive knowledge, skills and change of attitudes could be underestimated without applying the valid tools to test the reliability of the acquired comprehension of the learners in given learning and teaching materials.

Yet, educational evaluation is the continuous process that systematically and objectively assesses all the learning elements in practical terms of content delivery, learning quality and results to be achieved to determine the overall educational goals. The culture of evaluation and monitoring in the inclusive classroom is of general interest for both learners and teachers in an educational setting. It exemplifies standards, indicators, and shreds of evidence for evaluating culturally-proficient teaching and relevant learning outcomes. Such evaluation of learning and teaching activities are purposely designed for teacher's self-reflections and continuous improvement on teaching approaches and provision of constructive feedbacks by evaluators.

On the other hand, vigilantly monitoring is an ongoing process that regularly measures progress towards the goals and objectives of a prearranged educational program. It allows teachers to make changes during the learning cycle to ensure that teachers stay on a professional track in order to achieve their teaching philosophies. To some extent, monitoring ensures what has practically worked well or not. Whereas comprehensive evaluation checks the relevance, effectiveness, efficiency, impact, and sustainability of academic policy and strategies versus educational projects and programs. Indeed, monitoring and evaluation of the change in the learning environment will provide the information needed to determine whether the materials developed and instructional approaches used are academically appropriate and professionally stimulating. Importantly, continuous monitoring and evaluation are essential in providing the regularized flow of information needed for decision-making in educational settings. They can be used to identify the skill-building needs of those responsible for collecting data and preparing the reports.

Nominative and formative assessment of progress and

potential changing needs of learners is an overriding idea for the success of an educational program. Assessment of individual learning provides critical information to the principal stakeholders in the educational process, namely, the teachers, learners, and parents or guardians. The social gathering, analysis, and use of evaluation data that affect individual and collective progress will indicate how well an education system is answering the needs of the learners in particular and the societal expectations in general. This valuable information should be an integral part of the decision-making process for head teachers, classroom teachers, and other education personnel.

The terms formative and summative have become confusing in the past few years. By categorization, there are different types of assessments required by the school for quality education to be attained. On the one hand, formative assessment literally involves gauging ongoing progress by identifying learner strengths and apparent weaknesses. This form of valuation can also lead to greater learner achievement if both teachers and learners are able to reflect upon and actively use the information collected. Furthermore, if results are collected and analyzed properly, analysis information can also serve as a key driver in improving the teaching and learning process and quality standards. Formative assessments are time and again offered to be for learning because educators operate the results to modify and improve teaching techniques during an instructional period.

Nonetheless, summative assessments carefully evaluate academic achievement at the logical conclusion of an instructional period. This is substantially precise for formative assessment. Depending too frequently on one or the other and the reality of student achievement in your classroom becomes unclear. Formative Assessment is part of the instructional process. When incorporated into classroom practice, it provides the information needed to carefully adjust social teaching and learning while they are happening. In this sense, formative assessment informs both teachers and students about the student understanding at a point when timely adjustments can be made. These adjustments help to ensure students achieve targeted standards-based learning goals within a set time frame.

Although formative assessment strategies appear in a variety of formats, there are some distinct ways to distinguish them from summative assessments. One of the key components of engaging students in the determination of their own learning is providing them with descriptive feedback as they learn. In fact, research shows descriptive feedback to be the most significant instructional strategy to move them forward in their learning. Descriptive feedback provides students with a mutual understanding of what they are doing well, links to classroom learning, and gives specific input on how to gain the next step in the learning progression. On the other hand, summative assessments are typically scored and graded tests, assignments or projects used to determine whether students have learned what they were expected to learn during the defined instructional period.

Standardly, summative assessment represents an evaluation by examination or test. It is a formal evaluation of learners' competencies against established national or international learning objectives as identified in the national curriculum of modern education. This is typically performed at the ultimate end of the possible term or academic semester. Teachers and learners naturally devote more attention to what will be measured in form of tests or comprehensive examinations, and the results can inspire both parties to make improvements where they are needed. However, there are numerous assessment tools and approaches that when used effectively, can typically provide a direct indication of academic progress. Indeed, assessment drives instruction for quality education to be instantly realized.

By carefully checking with students throughout specific instruction, outstanding instructors constantly revise and refine their social teaching to comfortably accommodate the diverse needs of local students. Functional assessment can also drive effective learning and teaching activities. Evaluation practices must send the right signals to students about what to carefully study, how to study, and the relative time to typically spend on key concepts and necessary skills in a course. Accomplished ability to communicate clearly what they need to know and be able to do, both through a clearly articulated syllabus and by choosing assessments carefully to direct student energies.

Optimistically, academic expectations for learning result in students who rise to the rare learning occasions. Effective assessment typically provides students with a sense of what they know and don't know about a subject. If done well, the constructive feedback provided to students will indicate to them how to improve their academic performance. Assessments need to clearly match the content, the nature of thinking, and the social skills amply demonstrated in a class. Through constructive feedback from instructors, students become aware of their strengths and challenges with respect to course learning outcomes. It is significant to note an assessment done well should not be an amazement to learners, however, it should reflect on student accomplishments offered by the insights of the instructors into the effectiveness of their teaching strategies.

By systematically gathering, analyzing, and interpreting evidence we can determine how well student learning matches our possible outcomes and expectations for a lesson, unit, or course. The knowledge from feedback indicates to the instructor how to meaningfully improve instruction, where to strengthen teaching, and what areas are correctly understood and therefore may be cut back in future courses. In a balanced assessment system, both summative and formative assessments undoubtedly constitute an integral part of information gathering. One social distinction is to naturally think of formative assessment as standard practice. Formative assessment undoubtedly helps effective teachers to accurately determine the next steps during the learning process as the instruction approaches the summative assessment of a student learning. Another class distinction that underpins formative assessment correctly is student involvement. If prospective students are not involved in the evaluation process, formative assessment is not practiced or implemented to its maximum effectiveness. Students need to be involved both as assessors of their own learning and as valuable resources to other students. There are countless strategies teachers can implement to engage learners.

Along the direct line of educational aims, learning objectives identified in the official school curriculum and attitudinal change of lifelong learners should in common be in ideological conformity with the learning materials and teaching practices. Indeed, such a learning approach should be practically aligned to the assessment standards, flexible schedules and effective tools. It is equally substantial to use a variety of methods to assess learning outcomes to ensure that results reflect learning achievements with greater accuracy and responsibility in the education system. Indeed, monitoring and evaluation of learners' achievements at some points provide the information needed to control whether the teaching and learning process meets the needs of the individual and groups of learners.

On different account, it is domineering that different kinds of effective interventions such as policy change, awareness-raising campaigns. Indeed, community mobilization improves service delivery and response may need dissimilar kinds of policy frameworks, tools and indicators. The bottom line of monitoring and evaluation plays important role in the social system of education especially in academic policies, objectives, planning, and implementation. As such monitoring and evaluation are important to assess the social progress towards meeting learning objectives and progress of learners from one level to another. To operationalize quality observation and evaluation, it is necessary to identify the tools a teacher should use to carefully evaluate the quality of learning and teaching features.

Very much like quality education is highly emphasized, both monitoring and comprehensive evaluation should include relevant information on the cost of the program being monitored or evaluated. This allows judging the benefits of a program against its costs and identifying which intervention is needed, in terms of the most rapid rate of return. In the learning environment, reliable tools to carefully survey and assess extensive knowledge are carefully designed and regularly used by school personnel. These tools can either be under the social responsibility of the school management committee or the leading teacher of a given school. In its application, a designated instructor or mini-committee is embodied on a termly basis to conduct a number of surveys and observations in light of the progress of teaching and learning activities. In this respect, the committee or teacher visiting any classroom to assess teaching activities should provide a useful checklist for observation. This classroom checklist enables teachers or other school staff to record any behavioral learning between learners and the specific competency or incompetency of experienced teachers to deliver the content. In the face of crises, there could be many challenges students may face like stress, trauma, absenteeism of teachers and apparent inability to deliver the content effectively. Nonetheless, it is through in-classroom assessments in which several challenges can be identified and then well-thought-of during learning.

On the other hand, it is also imperative to give survey forms to learners either once a month or at the end of the term to provide feedback on their instructors' delivery technique and quality of learning. Furthermore, the teachers will be assigned the survey assessments to provide constructive feedback regarding the performance of the head teacher. In a similar fashion, learners will be given assessment forms to carefully evaluate the content and teachers based on the quality of delivery, appropriateness of the content, communication skills, just to mention a few. Out of what has been observed and surveyed, the monitoring indicators will be studied to understand the reality that can help the school leadership to carry out decisions. These monitoring indicators include a number of executed lesson plans, considerable number of used classroom materials, number of classroom visits by co-teacher, number of classroom visits by head teacher among others. The underlying reason for this kind of accurate assessment is to enable teachers and head teachers to be more active and complete their own duties on time.

Moreover, local students' attendance rates and end of term results, and overall performance will be good. During a visit of them to a classroom, a teacher will be encouraged and feel the urgency of taking his or her own classroom seriously with an organized lesson plan and scheme of works. On the contrary, it retells teachers' sincerity and dedication to the teaching profession. Bear in mind some instructors' sincerity to their duties; all the other teachers will be motivated and will tend to establish ownership of the learning activities. In this way, local ownership of teaching and learning will be developed among the teachers and head teachers to take responsibility for their actions as well as for their students' quality learning. Doing so will positively impact quality education and leadership development. Systematic monitoring will enable teachers to be sincerer with their teaching profession to improve their teaching. This also leads to the continuous improvement of learning and this also increases students' sincerity and interest in their study. Hence, typically generating a more enormous impact on local students' quality education.

As effective teachers' quality teaching is dependent on the meaningful feedbacks given by other colleagues through the monitoring the progress of teaching activities of staffs while they discharge their professional obligations. At some key points, if there are less sincerity and professional integrity among the staff, it negatively affects the smooth running of whole school. In an academic reality, an autonomous monitoring and evaluation system at any level of learning to get feedback from students and other cooperating teachers improves the teaching and learning processes in the face of crises. Teachers, on the other hand, can also conduct self-evaluations to determine the teaching needs and specific areas of fundamental weaknesses and strengths. This can also improve on good competent practices and teaching methods; hence, working on the appropriate learning materials and teaching aids. In the note, it equally considers the needs of psychosocial support for learners as an important factor for instantly realizing quality education in the familiar face of diplomatic and teaching crises.

It is imperative to carefully note that the core purpose of schooling is to improve the lives of children through the exceptional quality of teaching and learning so that every child can achieve their potential. In this sense, the school leaders and the wider teaching profession; therefore, have a responsibility to monitor the quality of teaching and learning activities throughout the learning system. Effective monitoring contributes to establish priorities for future improvement plans. This looks for all teachers to improve and accept that monitoring remains a key to support the improvement of the learning outcomes. Nonetheless, the main issue that faces local schools and staff to endure is the way in which monitoring is properly conducted and administered.

Monitoring is successful when the effective teachers feel empowered and gratefully accept personal responsibility for improving teaching and learning accomplishments. The monitoring process should be supportive and gently encourage academic staff to work collaboratively and cooperatively for the general good of all. Effective monitoring gently encourages successful collaboration and efficiently generates a cheerful atmosphere and supportive professional discussion. In the key point of remarkable fact, modern school naturally arise against the most convenient and most effective way to properly manage effective teacher and staff appraisals in all social conservatories. It typically serves as a comprehensive solution to empower teaching staff to unanimously uphold school improvement in practical terms of accurately portraying good character formation and professional integrity.

PART SEVEN

School Safety and Disaster Risk Reduction (DRR)

During emergency situations, education plays a critical role in helping children to cope with their particular situations and help them establish routines, normalize their lives, provide life-saving knowledge and skills for survival. Learners, responsible parents, and education personnel are repeatedly exposed to elevated risks during emergency situations. These may include threats to their emotional, social and nutritional well-being. This educational checklist will gently help educational personnel to monitor learning spaces such as access, necessary infrastructure, and teaching-learning environment and ensure that risks are typically reduced.

Possible disaster risk reduction (DRR) in common is the policy objective that is eagerly anticipated to progressively reduce to some considerable extent, potential risks caused by any possible emergency. The bottom-line reality is that DRR objectively explains in detail the proper course of actions designed to counteract any risks which have sufficiently shown multiple early warning mechanisms. DRR is also part and parcel of sustainable development and should be adequately incorporated in the development, humanitarian and educational activities.

As emergency strikes, catastrophes often follow the liens of inherent and manmade hazards. In this chapter, I talk earnestly about some of the manmade and natural blows which may have a negative impact on the lives of the community and the environment as well. As considerable time typically goes, there could in common be disaster risk as a direct result of the humanitarian crises. Factually, disaster risk is adequately expressed as the likelihood of loss of life, injury or destruction, and damage from a catastrophe in a given period of time.

Disaster risk is universally recognized as the possible consequence of the complex interaction between a potential threat and the unique characteristics that cause people and places vulnerable and exposed terribly. Put differently, there are many specific types of disasters such as flooding, fierce hurricanes, cyclones, drought, civil wars, community conflicts, just to prominently mention a few. In the historical context of South Sudan, flooding, famine, an outbreak of tropical diseases and man-made wars remain the most common destructive elements which have caused millions of lives and people's property over a long period of time.

In South Sudan, flooding has already created undesirable situations for both animals and human beings, especially in the local communities traditionally living in the low-lying areas. In the preceding years in Jonglei and Northern Bahr El Ghazal States, for rare instance, market places, residential areas, learning and administrative institutions, farms and public communication networks were completely submerged in water. As a direct result of the historic floods, more local institutions and people were superseded instantly by floods. One of the public schools called Jarwong Primary School in Bor South County, Jonglei State was completely water-logged until it was repositioned alongside the community to the more protected place.

In my account witnesses as sida Assistant Technical Programme Manager, the school alongside other 5 schools were directly supported by Save the Children through the adequate funding from Swedish International Development Cooperation Agency (Sida). Peculiarly, the school was voluntarily relocated from Jarwong residential area to protected Jopdoor area where TLS, a borehole, water containers, pit latrines, school fence were properly constructed from 2020 through 2022. In addition, the school was supported with assorted school supplies and teacher capacity training series of relative importance. In visible light of this great development support rendered to the troubled learners and the school community, it is worth-noting to thanks and appreciate Save the Children International in South Sudan. SCI is constantly and proactively involved in enthusiastically supporting affected children with educational activities and other child related referral pathways during emergency and non-emergency contexts. The support which I have justly observed on the ground have generated more enormous impacts in which more learners are enrolled and volunteer teachers recruited and given incentives and in-kind support. This typically implies that SCI in South Sudan has supported children to miraculously survive, typically learn and adequately protect their learning capacities during that specific flooding crisis in Bor South County, Jonglei State.

Undoubtedly, flooding is a predictable occurrence and man has very limited control over it. However, appropriate response and preparedness mechanisms ought to be put in place before any crises strike unexpectedly. In specific terms of manmade disasters, civil wars and inter-community conflicts cause ordinary reverses in South Sudan that seriously impact the social lives of the local people and their current environment. The negative impacts span from imminent death, injuries, loss of one's property as a result of cattle raiding, displacement of people and leaving of schools for the fear of the unknown.

On a similar note, a humanitarian catastrophe's severity depends on the level of destruction and how much an impact could create vulnerability on society and the school environment as well. In this respect, DRR is a systematic approach to positively identify, accurately assess and typically reduce the imminent dangers of disaster. Indeed, DRR is the systematic development and practical application of specific policies, effective strategies and standard practices that minimize potential vulnerabilities and disaster risks. To minimize and normalize the disasters at the community level, it is imperative that some risk mitigations can be devised and applied as quickly as possible to reduce the level of impact. One of the specific techniques to be typically used is to properly apply DRR in any emergency situations which may happen in the school setting. In this moral sense, disaster risk reduction is the policy objective of anticipating and reducing risk in whatsoever humanitarian assistance and preparedness are voluntarily given. In this respect, DRR may wisely be opted and applied squarely in all the troubled areas. This is not one-man show activity, but it seeks the support of all stakeholders including donors and the domestic government. In the local school setting, DRR aims to typically reduce the socio-economic vulnerabilities to disaster as well as dealing with the environmental and other hazards that typically trigger them.

DRR in common is an important variable, expected to lessen the damage caused by both natural and manmade activities like earthquakes, floods, droughts and cyclones, civil wars through an ethic of prevention. In the educational context, DRR is carefully considered a noble concept and practice of reducing disaster risks through systematic efforts to analyze and manage the causal factors of catastrophes such as reducing exposure to threats and lessening vulnerability of educational personnel, learners and school property. In an effort to normalize possible disasters, preparedness for backup responses, recovery, and reconstruction can reduce immediate losses caused by natural disasters and minimize the long-term social, economic, and environmental damages they caused. Emergency response can gently suggest the difference between life and death. Major natural disasters can and do have severe negative short-term and long-term economic and social impacts on the education system.

In a similar vein, disasters also appear to receive adverse longer-term consequences for low educational enrolment rate,

Capitalizing on Education in Emergencies in South Sudan

Pit Latrines in Jarwong Primary School in Bor South County, Jonglei State submerged in Water before relocating to high land (Courtesy of 2020)

Pit Latrines in Jarwong Primary School in Bor South County, Jonglei State after the relocating to high land (Courtesy of 2021)

shattered economic growth, diminished social development, and poverty reduction. The human population has been increasing at an exponential rate. With more local people, potential vulnerability progressively increases because there are more people to be affected by otherwise predictable and manmade events. Disaster mitigation measures are technically employed to eliminate or reduce the impacts and risks of hazards through proactive measures taken formerly and after the incident of an emergency. This depends upon concrete disaster management through the application of disaster preparedness, recovery and mitigation. It is virtually impossible to prevent natural and manmade disasters like those events caused by climatic and geological occurrences. This also applies to those disasters caused by the conflict of interests followed by the inevitable people to govern effectively.

Given the concentration of flooding, it is important that the government should introduce better flood warning systems to the households and the school authority. This reduces the intensity to expose the schools to disasters of any kind, lessening the vulnerability of people and property. This is also coupled with the enlightened management of land and the environment, and improving preparedness and early warning mechanisms for adverse events are all examples of disaster risk reduction. On this note, prevention should focus on preventing human hazards, primarily from potential natural disasters or manmade disasters such as terrorist attacks. While the other three components on the four phases of emergency management like preparedness, response and recovery are performed either in reaction to dangers or in anticipation of their consequences. On alleviation grounds, mitigation, on the other hand, measures risks and seeks to reduce the reasonable likelihood or consequences of hazard risk before an emergency ever strikes. Preparedness implies building and maintaining our incident command, and crisis action teams represent the focus of our preparedness activities to respond to any emergencies. Mitigation involves attempts to slow down the process of an event created by an emergency, usually by lowering the level of the incident to avoid collateral damage.

Typically taking proactive steps to reduce risk, also known as mitigation, helps reduce damage to homes, schools, and business centers may prevent loss of life. People also play an important role in lessening the impact of disasters by understanding their own risks and taking actions to minimize potential damage from hazards before they occur through a risk mitigation strategy. Mitigation strategy considers the goals, course of actions to be taken. The mitigation strategy is made up of three cores and required components such as mitigation goals, mitigation actions, and an action plan for implementation. These provide the framework to identify, prioritize and properly implement actions to reduce risk to vulnerabilities to the school community.

DRR is the strategic objective anticipated to reduce the extent of potential risks caused by any emergency. Precisely, it objectively explains in detail the course of actions designed to counteract any risks which have shown multiple early warning mechanisms. DRR is also part and parcel of sustainable development and should be seamlessly incorporated in the sustainable development and humanitarian activities per se.

As an emergency strikes, disasters often follow an inherent and manmade hazard. In the foregoing pages, I have talked clearly about some of the manmade and natural disasters which may have a negative impact on the lives of the community and the environment. As time goes, there could be disaster risk as a result of the crises. Factually, disaster risk is expressed as the likelihood of loss of dear life, injury or destruction, and damage from a disaster in a given period of time. Disaster risk is widely recognized as the consequence of the interaction between a threat and the characteristics that establish people and places vulnerable and exposed terribly.

Put differently, there are many specific types of disasters such as flooding, terrific hurricanes, cyclones, drought, civil wars, community conflicts, just to prominently mention a few. In the context of South Sudan, flooding, famine, an outbreak of tropical diseases and man-made wars are the most standard destructive elements which have caused millions of lives and people's property over a long period of time. Definitely, flooding has already created undesirable situations for both animals and human beings, especially in the communities living in low-lying areas. For instance, in Jonglei and Northern Bahr El Ghazal states, market places, residential areas, schools, and farms were submerged in water in the foregoing years, leading to the standard displacement of schools and the people. For certain, flooding is a natural occurrence and man has very limited control over it. Nonetheless, response and preparedness mechanisms ought to be put in place before any crises strike unexpectedly.

In terms of manmade disasters, civil wars and inter-community conflicts cause traditional disasters in South Sudan that seriously impact the lives of the people and their present environment. The negative impacts include death, injuries, loss of one's property as a result of cattle raiding, displacement of people, and abandonment of schools for the fear of the unknown. On a similar note, a disaster's severity depends on the level of destruction and how much an impact could typically create vulnerability on society and the school environment as well. In this respect, DRR represent a logical attitude to identify, assess and reduce the risks of disaster. Indeed, disaster risk reduction is the systematic development and practical application of specific policies, strategies and practices that minimize vulnerabilities and disaster risks. In order to minimize and normalize the disasters at the community level, it is imperative that some risk mitigations can be devised and applied as quickly as possible to reduce the level of impact.

One of the techniques to be used is to apply DRR since it is one of the policy objectives to anticipate and reduce risk in whatsoever assistance and preparedness which should be given. In this respect, a disaster risk reduction may wisely be opted and applied squarely in all the afflicted areas. This is not a one-man show, but it requires the assistance of all stakeholders including donors and the domestic government. In the school setting, DRR objects to minimize the socio-economic vulnerabilities to disaster as well as dealing with the environmental and other hazards that trigger them. As a means of providing a solution, DRR aims to mitigate the damage caused by both natural and manmade activities such as earthquakes, floods, droughts and cyclones, civil wars through an ethic of prevention.

In the educational context, DRR is carefully considered as a noble concept and practice of reducing disaster risks through systematic efforts to analyze and manage the causal factors of disasters like reducing exposure to threats and lessening vulnerability of educational personnel, learners and school property. In an effort to normalize disasters, preparedness for backup responses, recovery, and reconstruction can reduce immediate losses caused by natural disasters and minimize the long-term social, economic, and environmental damages they caused. Emergency response can mean the difference between life and death. Some catastrophic natural disasters may have severe negative short-term and long-term economic and social impacts on the education system.

In a similar vein, humanitarian disasters also appear to receive adverse longer-term consequences for low educational enrolment rate, shattered economic growth, diminished social development, and poverty reduction. The human population has been increasing at an exponential rate. With more people, potential vulnerability increases because there are more people to be affected by otherwise natural and manmade events. An ultimate issue to consider is that; mitigation measures of disasters are those that eliminate or reduce the impacts and risks of hazards through proactive measures taken before, during, and after the occurrence of an emergency. This requires concrete disaster management through the application of disaster preparedness, recovery, and mitigation. It is virtually impossible to prevent natural and manmade disasters such as those events caused by climatic and geological occurrences. This also applies to those disasters caused by the conflict of interests ensued by the inevitable people to govern effectively.

In practical terms of flooding, it is equally important that the government should introduce better flood warning systems to the residences and the school authority. This reduces the intensity to expose the schools to disasters of any kind, lessening the vulnerability of people and property. This is also coupled with the prudent management of land and the environment, and improving preparedness and early warning mechanisms for adverse events are all examples of disaster risk reduction. On this note, prevention should focus on preventing human hazards, primarily from potential natural disasters or manmade disasters such as terrorist attacks. While the other three components on the four distinct phases of emergency management such as preparedness, response and recovery are performed either in reaction to dangers or in anticipation of their consequences.

On the other hand, mitigation measures the risks and seeks to reduce the likelihood or consequences of hazard risk before an emergency ever strikes. Preparedness implies building and maintaining our incident command, and crisis action teams are the focus of our preparedness activities to respond to any emergencies. This involves logical attempts to slow the process of an event created by an emergency, usually by lowering the level of the occurrence. Gently taking proactive steps to cut risk, also known as mitigation, it helps to reduce destruction to homes, schools, and business centers may prevent loss of life. Likewise, affected people also play an important role to reduce the impact of disasters by understanding their own risks and taking actions to minimize potential damage from hazards before they occur through a risk mitigation strategy. Mitigation strategy considers the goals, course of actions to be taken. The mitigation strategy is made up of three cores with required components such as mitigation goals, mitigation actions, and an action plan for implementation. These provide the framework to identify, prioritize and implement actions to reduce risk to vulnerabilities to the school community.

In educational reality, the DRR in education accurately represent a logical approach to seamlessly integrate the functional analysis of disaster risks and disaster risk reduction measures in education sector development planning. Logically, DRR traditionally comprises of a combination of actions, processes and attitudes necessary for minimizing fundamental influences of unique vulnerability to improve the preparedness and positively enhance resilience of the education system. It generally empowers a never-ending development course of the modern education system and guarantees the continued access of all lifelong learners to quality education irrespective of race, specific gender, and socio-economic perspectives.

Temporary Learning Space (TLS) in Jarwong Primary School in Bor South County, Jonglei State submerged in Water before relocating to high land (Courtesy of 2020)

Temporary Learning Space (TLS) in Jarwong Primary School in Bor South County, Jonglei State after the relocating to higher land (Courtesy of 2021)

PART EIGHT

Conclusion and Personal Reflections

EiE represents a new field of study, which is yet to gain broader perspectives and institutional recognition in South Sudan. As a result of its low acknowledgement, the direction of the discipline and its primary importance is yet being underestimated. Needless to say, EiE, though it still lacks wider intellectual blessing, it is still dominant that the main function of EiE is to encourage the continuity of the learning and look for alternative funding and support toward education while people struggle with multiple means of solving emergencies. Education remains a fundamental right and a basic necessity for children caught up in humanitarian crises. It is key to give them a better future full hopes, develop their maximum potential, and equip them with skills and protection to restore their sense of normalcy and safety in their respective communities. In these regards, children become more self-sufficient and have a stronger voice on issues affecting them.

Given an unexpected strike of an emergency, pressing concerns to consider are the safety and security of learners, parents, school personnel, and protection of infrastructural stockpiles of the learning institutions. In addition, primary necessities and essential social and health services are highly needed to avert the situation in which learners and parents are exposed during crises. In the same line of thought, addressing the trauma of the children and school personnel is of paramount importance during crises. However, human and material resources are dedicated during the crises to support the defense and security sector, for this reason, leaving the education sector to suffer from the flow of limited resources to sustain the educational services. Given the fact the education is often underfunded or under budgeted, it is also one of the best tools for investing in peace, stability and socio-economic growth.

By cooperative advantage, EiE is a collective responsibility in which different development stakeholders are expected to participate in the provision of quality education either morally, financially, materially, or in other forms. On humanitarian grounds, EiE should focus on strong partnerships and synergic efforts to instantly realize rapid, efficient, effective, and innovative education response. To conceptualize the big educational agenda to be applied during emergency contexts, it is imperative the schooling should continue and access be guaranteed throughout the year. This should be supported with learning materials, which are made relevant to the contexts of the communities at all levels of education in South Sudan. In this sense, I elaborate more in these couples of chapters about the roles of the communities, education actors, and the school authorities in complementing the commitment of the domestic government to address educational issues in times of emergencies.

Provision of educational opportunities during crises continues to be a disturbing challenge being faced by the fragile states. It is believed that education acts as a catalyst for peacebuilding and conflict moderation in all its informative aspects. In an emergency context, establishing safe and secure environments for teachers and learners remain the priority. Henceforth, creating safe spaces where social and emotional needs are addressed and academic routines are monitored. Such establishments of protective learning spaces are meant to help them recover from traumatic events for being in a situation that has impacted their physical and mental well-beings. This requires a training phase that focuses primarily on preparations with psychosocial content.

Routinely, education for all is a firm international commitment and collective goal for all members of the United Nations across the globe. Under this legal provision and social commitment, to implement education for all, the United Nations' Agencies, domestic governments, NGOs, religious-based groups, Civil Societies and other members of the communities are voluntarily and legitimately indebted to encourage and support education during the emergency and non-emergency situations. As a result of the denial of educational opportunities to the population or certain sections of the community, crises and instability continue to deepen across the affected group of people in a given country.

In reality check, education is all about life-sharing. To such a degree, the values of education should be contextually relevant to community needs and continually delivered to appreciate the quality of learning across different geographic and demographic entities. In my personal opinion regarding the provisions of EiE, I adhere to the view that the government is not willing and committed to delivering quality educational services to the citizens. Education being one of the absolute human rights, every vulnerable person is entitled to, and all school-age-going children should gain unhindered and similar access to determining opportunities. To approach this, it will pave the way for a viable education system where genuine knowledge, practical skills, enlightened attitudes, and diversified societal values will be instilled into the minds of the learners at all levels of education. In doing so, the brilliant students should be admitted to the College of Education in the public and private institutions of higher learning to attain relevant education for quality teaching. Since education is not for weak and low-level-minded individuals in society, it is overbearing that we aim at education toward citizens who think outside the box like global citizens. This is to enable them to note things in a more strategic answerability of the problem and sort out the realistic frames of references for practical solutions.

Administratively, an effective forecasting for school activities remains the hardcore component of effective school management during crises. Along this line of rationality, this educational planning episode is executed by the school leadership in which all the staff is directed to goals and guided to project for the success of the school. This is through the application of effective monitoring and evaluation of the social and academic progress of learners. In this respect, persistent planning and effective management of teacher professional development and the content being delivered should be prioritized and attained in the earnest commitment. On the other hand, I passionately believe that South Sudan needs a strong and reformed educational agenda in which the current problems facing education should be called by their real names and their basic originalities.

By calling it by its real description, I mean problems facing the operationalization of the education system like widespread corruption, employment of incompetent personnel, diversion of public funds, malpractices in examinations, poor learning environment, inadequate and poorly furnished learning facilities, just to mention a few. This may pave the way for the re-establishment of the strong academic background and professional abilities of the learners who will remain open-minded and well-informed with zero tolerance to corruption and other forms of school maladministration. This practically breeds quality education at all levels of schooling.

In the context of South Sudan and elsewhere in the war-affected regions, the role of the governments is obvious as underscored in the domestic and international laws. From the perspectives of domestic laws, the legally binding instruments have primarily remained in principle without being practically implemented. In this sense, South Sudan needs an Education System where schooling is made compulsory and universal at all levels of education. Principally, it needs an education system in which both boys and girls have equitable and unhindered access to educational opportunities during the crisis and non-emergency contexts. As defined by the need to intervene during crises, EiE focuses on both short-term and long-term aspects.

In light of worthwhile aspect, long-term quality education focuses on the construction of post-construction societies. However, short-term aspect of EiE should strategize on the commonness of peace for social cohesions, protection and safety of learners and their parents, and the continuity of learning in all aspects of current needs. In my view, the coordinated character of the domestic governments, community and locally-based organizations, donor agencies, and international humanitarian organizations, interest groups, and religious-based clusters can provide and support relaxed access to educational services that are of reasonable quality. By doing so, may lead the nation-states to realize the INEE Minimum standards designed to address the issues of EiE in South Sudan in particular and generally in the world over. As such, I envision an education system where economically disadvantaged children, children with disabilities (CwD), as well as children from minority groups, retain equal access to teaching and learning opportunities across the country.

Apparently, in every country that intends to improve the efficiency and effectiveness of its social, economic, and cultural domains in the face of crises, it must consider the active involvement and participation of the community members. This is because members of the community have resources and ideas to be invested in education to realize quality education at all levels of learning. In this sense, the members of the community are more willing to devote any kind of support once they are involved in the decision-making process and this enables them to own the learning processes and support proactive activities of the school. Given the fact that education remains the collective responsibility for all, EiE envisions the system where non-discrimination of both genders is eliminated.

To supplement these practical initiatives, it is vital that South

Sudan needs an Education System where 35% of the fiscal year budget is allocated to the education sector to account for the operational costs as well as paying the fat salaries of the school personnel. This will minimize the desertion of the teaching profession by the qualified teaching force in search of green pastures outside their appropriate fields of employment. However, the roles supposed to be rendered to the country by members of the community are so far not realizable due to the fact that the government at times undervalues the position of the ordinary community members. Idiosyncratically, this is precise in the context of developing countries like South Sudan where roles of the community are largely undermined. This is in fact, the case in South Sudan where the role of the community needs-based associations, school management committees, PTAs, and other education stakeholders are not validly given due attention both in the private and public learning institutions.

Since the community members are not fully mobilized to be part of the education system, they maintain their distance and watch the unfolding events of educational activities during crisis context. Being ignored by the government could cause them feel less concerned and they opt not to take any responsive measures in that respect. As such, this may render community roles to be least effective for that matter. It is worth mentioning that education is a collective responsibility that depends upon the inputs and support of everyone in the community.

At some points, quality, accessibility, and affordable education can be nothing, but could be achieved during crises when the peace initiatives and conflict mitigation mechanisms are put in place by the government and its peace partners. This will foster an enabling learning environment that accommodates the needs and aspirations of diverse members of society in a peaceful atmosphere. Creating an encouraging environment can pave the way for establishing self-reliant and self-sustainable societies. For this reason, EIE encourages counseling activities to be applied on daily basis in order to create a trusting relationship and safe learning, and supportive environment for learners and teachers. This generates them to freely enjoy their learning activities without fear or intimidation.

On the other extreme, a teacher is a core component in some educational settings. So, South Sudan as a new and underdeveloped country needs an education system where qualified manpower is employed and deployed on the basis of merits and not on tribal or family leagues. Taking into consideration the professional merits as the basis for employment of leaders can ensure the delivery and acquisition of quality education with regards to determining outcomes of the 6 Cs of the *21st Century skills. These core 21st century skills include Character Education, Good citizenship, Creativity, Collaboration, Communication, and critical reasoning skills*. Without emphasizing and implementing strategies to achieve these 6 Cs, then the education system is critically wounded.

In South Sudan, citizens absolutely need an Education System where TPD centers are established right from national to state levels. Not only providing physical facilities, however but they should also be fully furnished to upgrade the competent knowledge and teaching skills of teachers through pre-service and in-service training opportunities. Along that line of thought, it is imperative that citizens need an education system where the brain drained South Sudanese personalities are morally encouraged and financially supported to return home. This can enable them to be engaged and maintained professionally to expedite their skilled leverages and intellectual synergies for the benefit of this exceptional nation.

With regards to tertiary education, South Sudan needs an Education System where research and particularly action-oriented research studies are practically encouraged and enthusiastically supported through university market collaboration. This will encourage the country to align its innovative work with state-of-the-art career pathways for the improvement of socio-economic growth and social progress. In addition, we need an Education System where admission to public and private institutions of higher learning is based on academic abilities rather than on the basis of the gun class directives and political influence. However, this could only be possible through encouraging a system where qualified manpower is employed on the basis of merits and not on tribal or family unions.

On the other hand, it is at present a habitual datum that malpractices in the final examinations and leakages of study results have some negative bearings not only on the national system of education, but also at the individual and professional levels. In this background, it should be admitted that South Sudan needs a system where qualified and experienced examiners are recruited on equal diversity and on professional virtues. In consideration of quality-based educational standards, employing and deploying trained teachers countrywide to set and mark final examinations both at primary and secondary school levels will enhance the quality of education standards.. In this way, it will minimize widespread leakage of examination questions and answers into the local markets. Hence, improving the quality of education at all levels of education in the country.

As internationalization and globalization are widening their horizons in diverse sectors, South Sudan as a country really needs a system where cross-border collaborations are encouraged. Supporting cross-regional teamwork in the education sector should be through regional and global university partnerships, professional cooperation and collaborative exchange of learning and knowledge among the professional communities. This may encourage the flow of expertise, knowledge, and skills that can help the country catch up with the rest of the work morally, financially, socially, educationally, and economically. Many scholars have argued that crucial phases of teaching should focus much on training with psychosocial content and basic pedagogy.

In professional reality, this may support teachers to shift the content of the training from psychosocial support services to inclusive and fair gender sensitivity teaching methodologies. This pedagogical stage will support teachers to engage in their professional development and exploits present resources to provide an engaged, active, and conducive learning environment for all. On the same note, it teaches to demonstrate a more proper understanding of positive and alternative discipline approaches to manage student behaviors more effectively. In fact, the teacher is capable to create a learning and gender-fair environment, and non- discriminate as well as demonstrating a clear understanding of creating daily routines and procedures using various teaching and learning aids to engage learners meaningfully and suitable to class size. As he or she is familiar with child development, the teacher develops higher-order thinking skills through the application of inquiry and questioning techniques for effective learning exercises.

Since teaching methods are changing the practical gears towards the 21st century, it is imperative that teaching approaches ought to emphasize the delivery of quality educational services to learners. This should also be on the basis of applying problem-based approaches and experiential learning domains in a non-threatening and inclusive learning environment. In so doing, can help to reduce the barriers to quality education such as discriminatory behaviors towards girl education, gender-based violence and the socio-economic situation at family levels. In the informative context, South Sudan is a country with very limited or poor learning facilities, and access is also hindered by several internal and external factors. To address some of these challenges, the first-ever step is to provide temporary learning spaces especially in areas where there is the displacement of schools. Along that line of support, the provision of basic health and nutritional services may also add greater weight to the learning domain in the face of crises.

In an effort to realize EiE, advancing the nationwide Mobile Schooling Initiatives among the Pastoral Communities could be a worthwhile goal. Mobile school is an emerging type of learning which is aimed at increasing access to education for children and adults. This is based on the provision of culturally and religiously appropriate basic education to children who would otherwise find it difficult to access formal education in their respective communities. Since South Sudan is a country overwhelmed in poverty and a high rate of illiteracy can deserve such educational opportunities to be provided during crises.

The mobile school system for pastoral communities has been exclusively given no attention during the emergency and non-emergency situations. In the context of South Sudan, pastoral communities include Nuer, Dinka, Murle, Mundari, Taposa, Atuot, just to mention a few, who primarily depend on traditional subsistence farming activities for survival, which is obvious for the poor yields. In fact, there is a high rate of illiteracy among these communities, unlike other communities in South Sudan. As emergency strikes, the situation in light of education is worsened by limited access to learning opportunities in the war-affected communities. Some of these communities are occasionally on the move during the spell of the dry season in search of pastures and water for their cattle.

In the course of their movement and settlement in different places, it is obvious that violent conflicts could happen among themselves on the one hand, and with the host communities, on the other hand. So providing them with mobile schooling may reduce native impressions of conflict that could lead to instability and a high rate of education in their respective communal boundaries. As such, being coupled with a lack of educational opportunities, conflicts among these communities continue to be pervasive and rampant. The most striking examples with frequent communal conflicts include some sections of Warrap, Unity, Western Bahr el Ghazal, Jonglei, and Lakes states.

In the same vein, communal conflicts extended to part of Twic, Gogrial West and Gogrial East Counties with cattle raiders from Unity State in the recent years of confrontation which claimed hundreds of lives in Gogrial State, as well as Murle versus Dinka Bor, Nuer versus Murle, to mention them. Primarily, the Dinka and Nuer, two rival pastoralist groups, have overtime competed over grazing land and water points for their cattle in the past. These tribal clashes have usually taken place in a local context with many massive amounts of fatalities experienced on both sides so far. Among other communities which have been embroiled in inter-sectional conflicts, much of the learning activities has become pretentious in the watch of the government and other education stakeholders across the country.

In the same lines, most of the nomadic youths are so hostile and only believe in fighting and winning wars over the others. Presumably, the youth perceives the notion of fighting to be portraying their superiority, gallantry, and strengths over their opponents. As a result of frequent conflicts, loss of lives and destruction of property have sporadically become the order of the day in different parts of South Sudan. With the high rate of illiteracy in the country, it is now apparent that the lack of an organized education system in form of an Alternative Education System (AES) out of the mainstream system exacerbates widespread illiteracy. Indeed, this is the major contributing factor to communal and tribal conflicts that have barely hit the country here and now. To confront educational challenges facing pastoral communities, it is wise to change the mindsets of the armed youths from traditional ways of doing things to modern life.

In modern times characterized by civilization and socialization, this requires investing heavily and strategically in education to realize rapid and sustainable development both at national and local levels. This is in line with the three pillars of the World Bank Group Education Strategy of 2020, which are passionately put clear as it to invest early, invest smartly, and invest for all. So investment in education requires immediate actions and response to be applied elegantly for the common good of all. In the words of great iconic statesman Nelson Mandela, *"Education is the most powerful weapon you can use to change the world."* His popular quotation has been adopted and advanced far and wide by education actors and partners to encourage humankind to undertake education exclusively. This is also in line with the commitment of the UN Agencies and other international organizations who posit that education promotes peaceful and inclusive societies as well as preventing conflicts and heals their immediate consequences.

Given the necessity to provide education for all, I have always believed that most nomadic communities are unenlightened and not fully sensitized about the importance of education and peaceful coexistence among themselves and with their hosts. Since the government is the sole provider of basic services (education as inclusive precedence), my view is that all must access equal educational opportunities irrespective of the challenges the country has been going through for the last decades of peace and successive wars. In the event that nomadic communities are denied their right to basic education, this noticeably suggests that they are socially and culturally denied their basic rights to life. Hence, the end result is they are economically disadvantaged and professionally disconnected from the rest of the societies. Conversely, economists and public commentators, may agree with me from an economic viewpoint that most of the economic activities are detectably undermined by frequent communal conflicts. From a social outlook, it may be mentioned that education remains the foundation for producing informed and productive citizens. In reality, an all-inclusive education approach that considers pastoral education as an alternative means to reduce illiteracy in the country could be the best alternative for combating illiteracy and communal conflicts.

In other words, it will shape their attitudes by instilling in their minds the positive social values that encourage peaceful coexistence and socio-economic transformation. Essentially, systemized pastoral education is a huge task to be accomplished, but it is necessary for the government to take it as an action point to organize and support education countrywide. Viewing it from the perspectives of the human rights domain, education is treated as a basic right to which everyone is entitled to including the nomadic youth. In fact, many of them still think that South Sudan has not gained independence since the lack of educational opportunities for their children remains the first and foremost challenge. Although pastoral education activities seem to be less effective in this context, it is crucial for eradicating illiteracy and attaining quality education for a quality life. On the positive side, education distinctively contributes to the acquisition of positive social values at individual and community levels in all spheres of life. In this sense, I am convinced that advancing a competency-based curriculum that provides equal educational prospects for all is the only viable solution to be given due attention.

Equally important, pastoral education initiatives can be communicated across cultural lines with more focus to develop independent-mindedness of the nomadic youths with regards to the pursuit of professional knowledge and skills. Basically, this may meet the goal of a culturally responsive curriculum that respects and acknowledges the cultures of the nomadic communities. However, the design of pastoral education in the context of community cultures should not in a sharp manner contradict the national and legal laws. Because community values should be respected in the light of the application of national laws and international principles. This calls for preliminary consultation with the members of the community on how education for all can be approached and achieved.

On the other hand, advancing basic education services in rural settings in form of mobile schooling is more cost-effective to reform the national education agenda. This can add a beneficial heavyweight improvement to the achievement of literacy and numeracy goals at the national level. It is equally important to observe that pastoral education is the feasible alternative to disseminate the true meaning of intellectual capital to the mindsets of the youths. Adequately, this may prepare them to access knowledge and skills to enable them to become productive and informed citizens to steer their country forward socio-economically and sustainably. In so doing will heighten the educational reality that the more they are educated, the more they can access vital messages and life-sustaining information for survival, safety, and protection. The functionality of the school-based learning approach is universally accepted in South Sudan to some extent, however, the mainstream education system is still weak.

In this respect, I still maintain that the weak education system largely ignores the mobile schooling strategy that can be applied to engage nomadic communities actively and constructively. In a clearly inclusive term, education should be made accessible, affordable, and even-handed for all within the application of a non-discriminatory approach. Despite the government's commitment to implement universal education for all, the policy goes on a theory because of a lack of practical execution and specific strategies like mobile schooling for the nomadic communities could be incorporated to engage and benefit them for the common good of their one-to-one communities. Habitually, some education partners and actors have been talking about the possibility of initiating and adopting mobile schooling initiatives. Yet, no concrete success has been achieved. Literally, these young graduates, which are loitering here and there are resourceful in this regard as they could be recruited as teachers and mobile school administrators. To realize affirmative learning outcomes, these teachers could be substantially motivated to mastermind the teaching job. At this moment, it may be admitted that the underutilized fresh graduates could be trained to use the most progressive methods available to impart knowledge to the beneficiaries for the common good of the country. This will also reduce the number of unemployed youths who are vulnerable to recruitment to different armed groups fighting for their self-interests and promotion of their ideological egocentricities at different social and political scales.

With emergency situations striking, in an unexpected manner, it is imperative to say that education in emergencies is a vibrant tool to change the face of socio-economic and technological structures in the country. Specifically, emergencies may strike terribly in war-affected countries or regions and this calls for a holistic approach to provide quality and accessible education for all the learners. So, the bottom line is the best educational opportunities should be strategically aligned with national educational goals and enthusiastically received by the beneficiaries to develop individual talents and personalities. In a similar vein, faculty and staff members may benefit from instruction in crisis response, in terms of quality teaching, and other forms of professional development. This points to the fact that learning activities may continue undisturbedly even when emergencies strike. Specifically, it is an important phantom for the government and the wider community to keep schools functioning during crises.

On the other hand, viewing it from an angle of gender equality, girl education is factually disregarded in rural settings. In this context, it is obvious that girls are ostensibly considered to be the source of wealth in terms of pride price. In this respect, girls are the most marginalized groups, since they are the ones to take care of the domestic chores and brothers and sisters within the campsites. Hence, chances of keeping girls out of school are very high, and this alone discriminates against their rights to education. For obvious roles assigned to them, girls, specifically, have been on move from one place to another in search of water and food as well as clearing out the cow dungs from the camp yard. In fact, when educational opportunities are brought closer to their vicinity in form of mobile schooling, they will learn and benefit from key messages for building a sustainable life and change of mindsets and bad community attitudes. Though I concede the government has recently initiated such learning opportunities, however, they were not implementable. Most importantly, there has been a low intensification of awareness-raising campaigns at the grassroots level and particularly in the cattle camps to enlighten them about the wider educational prospects. To this respect, I still insist that much has not been done adequately since transitioning nomadic youth from cattle camp life to modern town life has been long overdue.

Though sensitizing them through the practical approach to disseminate knowledge is looming, there is a need to establish a bilateral understanding with the local leaders who are the immediate front-runners to whom they could pay more allegiance than the central government. In a similar vein, it depends upon the inclusion of bureaucratic education departments and their line ministries at both local and national levels. This may enable unhindered and stress-free access to accomplish educational goals. Since there are diverse and dynamic nomadic communities across South Sudan, it is wise to provide education uniformly, quantitatively, and qualitatively on the basis of their respective locations. This will definitely provide a conducive and understanding environment for young men and women to collectively think that education is the most effective tool to improve their lives socially, economically, and intellectually.

The complexity of social attitude to learning and the dimension of implementing pastoral education at a given period of time and space have complicated the holistic schooling during crises. As such, this may require aligned cooperation from other education actors in the country to build and strengthen the coordinated synergies. At this point, offering and availing educational activities will keep them busy engaged academically.

Consequently, this will create positive social impacts among the pastoral youths in their respective communities. In a nutshell, capitalizing on pastoral education implies investing in human resource development for building sustainable and peaceful communities. In light of these factual outlooks, availing of educational opportunities, recruiting teachers, and providing medical services would liberate the nomadic youth from illiteracy, poverty, insecurity, and poor health conditions. So education in emergencies is a collective responsibility that calls for realistic approaches and performance so as to realize holistic education, that is sustainably responsive and professionally appealing to community needs and expectations.

GLOSSARY

Assessment: The practical term is typically referred to as an extensive investigation carried out before planning educational activities and intervening in an emergency to determine needs and apparent gaps in the response of available resources.

Career Guidance: This typically refers to any services and activities intended to encourage individuals of any age and at any point of learning throughout their lives, to make educational, training, and occupational choices and to manage their career pathways effectively.

Child Soldier: This refers to an individual, typically below the age of 18, but often younger, in the armed forces of the state or an armed group.

Child-Centered Learning: This traditionally refers to specific instruction and learning processes that are designed around the possible experiences, skills, knowledge, and interests of the children.

Child-Friendly Environment: This refers to a supportive educational and inclusive, healthy, friendly, protective, and rights-based community environment.

Child-Friendly School: This in common is a school where the physical, social, psychological, spiritual, and intellectual needs of the child are met.

Civil Society: This is a term for a broad array of non-governmental and nonprofit groups that help their society at a large function while working to advance their own or others' social wellbeing.

Conflict: This refers to any situation in which armed violence over government or territory emerges and disrupts the lives and livelihoods of citizens.

Conflict Mitigation: This refers to robust action and processes aimed at addressing underlying causes of conflict and improve the way that those involved act and perceive the issues.

Conflict-affected States: *These refer to those conflict-prone states with fragile institutions and low capacities to deliver quality services and provide general protection.*

Context: *This is the set of facts or extraordinary circumstances that instantly surround a specific situation or historical event.*

Counseling: *This typically refers to a process in which the counselor assists a client to require interpretations of facts relating to a situation, make informed choices, plan and implement the best option that fits him or her.*

Curriculum: *This typically refers to the selection and organization of a learning system with specific goals, contents, strategies, measurement, and resources, and experiences for students is important for their personal and community development.*

Demobilization: *This refers to the process by which parties to a conflict disband their military structures and combatants initiate the transformation into civilian life.*

Disarmament, Demobilization, and Reintegration (DDR): *This is the gradual process of disarming soldiers or other fighters, disbanding their military units and keep them integrated socially and economically into society by finding civilian livelihoods.*

Disaster Risk Reduction (DRR): *This refers to the systematic approach, employed to identify, assess and reduce the risks of disaster when emergency strikes.*

Disarmament: *This the collection of small arms, light and heavy weapons within a conflict zone.*

Education: *This is the possible transfer of necessary knowledge, skills, favorable attitudes, and positive values from one key generation to the other through training, research, teaching, and mentorship.*

Educational Measurement: *This refers to the science and practice of getting information about characteristics like their knowledge, skills, abilities and interests.*

Emergency: *This refers to an expected hostile situation that leads to the loss of human and material lives, either caused by human activities or occurs naturally in a given environment.*

Fragile States: *These refer to those states, which maintain weak institutions and low capacities to typically deliver quality and fair policies as well as being part of the problem in marginalizing the minorities.*

Gender Balance: *This is the proportionate representation of women and men at all levels in all areas.*

Gender Equality: *This refers to the state where people of all genders have equitable rights, responsibilities, and opportunities without stating any distinction.*

Gender: *This refers to specifically and socially constructed roles and relationships, stable personality traits, prevailing attitudes, behaviors, moral values, relative power, and influence that society ascribes to the two sexes on a differential basis.*

Gender-Based Violence: *Typically refers to the violence directed against individuals or groups on the basis of their gender or sex.*

Good Governance: *This traditionally refers to promote equity, participation, pluralism, transparency, accountability and the rule of law, in a manner that is effective, efficient, and enduring.*

Human Rights: *These refer to the basic prerogatives and freedoms to which all humans are entitled to.*

Human Security: *This typically means protecting the vital core of all human lives in ways that enhance fundamental freedom and human fulfillment.*

Inclusive Education: *This refers to a process of addressing and typically responding to the diversity of needs of all learners through increasing participation in learning, cultures, communities, and reducing exclusion from education and from within the education system.*

Indicators: *These are measurable qualitative and quantitative data, which aim to identify change, achievements, and impacts.*

In-service Training: *This refers to the continued training opportunities given to teachers after they have begun teaching in classrooms.*

Measurement: *This refers to the action of measuring something to control its worth, position and value.*

Man-made Emergencies: *This refers to man-made activities that can affect both human lives and substantial assets.*

Natural Emergencies: *This is a momentous adverse event resulting from logical processes of the Earth such as floods, hurricanes, tornadoes, volcanic eruptions, earthquakes, tsunamis, storms, and other geologic processes.*

Peace Education: *This refers to mean contextually responsive instruction that energetically promotes mutual understanding and functional analysis of possible conflict, its causes, and ways of invariably responding to it without harm.*

Peacebuilding: *This refers to the context of post-conflict recovery efforts to promote reconciliation and reconstruction.*

Pre-service Training: *This traditionally refers to the training teachers receive before entering a classroom and beginning to teach after graduation from a given profession.*

Quality Education: *Typically refers to education that is informative, child-friendly, desirable, affordable, accessible, and sensitive to lifelong learners' gender, diversity, culture, and language.*

Reintegration: *This refers to the process, which allows ex-combatants and their families to admirably adapt, economically and socially, to a productive life.*

Relevant Education: *This refers to the learning and either directly applicable experiences to the personal aspirations, interests, or cultural experiences of students connected in some way to the real-world issues, problems and contexts.*

School Environment: *This is the social-emotional climate of the school that reflects the quality and character of school life like norms, goals, values, interpersonal relationships, teaching and learning practices, and organizational structures.*

Security Sector: *This refers to the responsible sanctuary sector for protecting the state and communities within the state.*

Sexual Exploitation and Abuse (SEA): *This refers to the economic exchange of money, shelter, food, or other goods for sex or sexual favors for someone in a vulnerable position and threatening or forcing someone to have sex or provide sexual favors under forced conditions.*

Sexual Violence: *This is a form of gender-based violence and refers to any act, attempt, or threat of a sexual nature that results, or is likely to result in, physical or psychological harm.*

Teacher Training: *This typically refers to the national education policies, specified procedures, and provisions premeditated to equip teachers with the relevant knowledge, attitudes, behaviors, and skills they require to perform their tasks effectively in the classroom, school settings, and in the wider community.*

Trauma: *This is an emotional response to very distressing events or possible experiences. It is a genuine feeling that occurs after one has been exposed to life-threatening experiences, which can lead to fear, loneliness, despair, stress, etc.*

Violence: *This is the intentional use of physical force or power, threatened, or actual, against oneself, another person, or against the group or local community that either result in or consider a high likelihood of resulting in injury, death, physiological harm, and deprivation.*

War-affected Areas*: Refer to those geographical areas that are impacted by violent and armed conflict, which result to massive displacement of local people, potential loss of lives, widespread insecurity, and destruction of intellectual property.*

REFERENCES

Burde D, Guven O, Kelcey J, Lahmann H, Al-Abbadi K (2015). *What Works to Promote Children's Educational Access, Quality of Learning, and Wellbeing in Crisis-Affected Contexts? Education Rigorous Literature Review.* Department for International Development.

Cahill, K., (2010). *Even in Chaos: Education in Times of Emergencies. New York*: Fordham University Press.

Cole, A.E. (2007). *Teaching the Violent Past: History Education and Reconciliation.* USA: Rowman & Littlefield Publishers Ltd.

Culbertson, S., & Constant, L. (2015). *Education of Syrian Refugee Children: Managing the Crisis in Turkey, Lebanon, and Jordan.* Rand Corporation.

Education Cannot Wait (2018-2021). ECW Strategy 2018-2021: *Advancing Gender Equality in Education in Emergencies.* Retrieved from www.educationcannotwait.org

Education Cluster (2012). *South Sudan Minimum Standards for Education in Emergencies. Juba:* Ministry of General Education and Instructions.

Gurtong Peace Trust (2018). *New and Current Map of the Republic of South Sudan.* Juba: Retrieved from www.gurtong.net

Hammond, H. (2013). Language of Instruction for Increased Access to Relevant Education for Conflict Affected Children in South Sudan. *Journal of International Affairs Review*, 21(2).

Hayes, A., Turnbull, A., and Moran, N. (2018). *Universal Design for Learning to Help All Children Read: Promoting Literacy for Learners with Disabilities (First Edition).* Washington, D.C.: USAID.

Jok, J. M. (2011). *Diversity, Unity, and Nation Building in South Sudan.* Washington, DC: US Institute of Peace.

Linda, D. (2006). *Powerful Teacher Education: Lessons from Exemplary Programs*. San Francisco: Jossey-Bass.

Lisa, L., L. (2012). *Trauma Counseling: Theories and Interventions. New York*. Spring Publishing Company. LLC.

Mayai, A. T., & Hammond, H. (2014). *The Impacts of Violence on Education in South Sudan. Policy Brief. Juba, South Sudan:* The Sudd Institute.

McEvoy, C., & LeBrun, E. (2010). *Uncertain future: Armed Violence in Southern Sudan*. Geneva: Small Arms Survey.

Muggah, R., & Berman, E. (2001). *Humanitarianism under Threat: The Humanitarian Impacts of Small Arms and Light Weapons*. Small Arms Survey.

Mundy, K. & Sarah Dryden-Peterson, S., (2011). *Educating Children in Conflict Zones: Research, Policy and Practice for Systemic Change. New York*: Teachers' College Press.

Nicolai, S. (2003). *Education in Emergencies: A tool kit for starting and managing Education in Emergencies*. London: Save the Children UK.

Prem, C., P. (2005). *Development of Higher Education in India. New Delhi: Shree Publishers & Distributors*. SA Journal of Human Resource Management. Vol. 6 No. 2 pp. 32 – 41. Retrieved from http://www.sajhrm.co.za

Samman, E., Lucci, P., Jessica, H., Bhatkal, T., Amanda, R., Nicolai, S., Stuart, E., and Caron, C., (2018). SDG progress: *Fragility, Crisis and Leaving No One Behind Report. Overseas Development Institute*.

Sidhu, K. (2005). *New Approaches to Measurement and Evaluation*. New Delhi: Sterling Publishers Private Limited.

Smith, A. (2009) *Education and Conflict. Think piece prepared for the Education for All Global Monitoring Report 2011 The Hidden Crisis Armed conflict and education*. Education for All, Global Monitoring Report. UNESCO Paris. 21 pp. Research report. Retrieved from http://unesdoc.unesco.org/images/0019/001913/191338e.pdf

Sommers, M. (2004). *Co-Coordinating Education during Emergencies and Reconstruction: Challenges and Responsibilities.* International Institute for Educational Planning (IIEP) UNESCO. 7-9 rue Eugene-Delacroix, 75116 Paris, France.

South Sudan General Education Act (2012). *General Education Act, 2012. Juba:* Ministry of Justice and Constitutional Affairs.

United Nations Office for the Coordination of Humanitarian Affairs (OCHA, (2018). *Humanitarian Bulletin South Sudan, Issue 8. Juba: Author.* Retrieved from www.reliefweb.int/ www.unocha.org/ south-sudan

Vaessen, J. Diaz, A., Ekaterina, S. & Arushi, M. (2016). *Crisis-Sensitive Education Sector Planning: UNESCO-IIEP Support in South Sudan.* Juba: UNESCO.

www.ingramcontent.com/pod-product-compliance
Lightning Source LLC
Chambersburg PA
CBHW030253010526
44107CB00053B/1700